A(ZX)103

An Introduction to the Humanities

The Open University

The Colosseum

Block 2

This publication forms part of an Open University course A(ZX)103 *An Introduction to the Humanities*. Details of this and other Open University courses can be obtained from the Student Registration and Enquiry Service, The Open University, PO Box 197, Milton Keynes, MK7 6BJ, United Kingdom: tel.+44 (0)870 333 4340, email general-enquiries@open.ac.uk

Alternatively, you may visit the Open University website at http://www.open.ac.uk where you can learn more about the wide range of courses and packs offered at all levels by The Open University

To purchase a selection of Open University course materials visit http://www.open.ac.uk, or contact Open University Worldwide, Michael Young Building, Walton Hall, Milton Keynes MK7 6AA, United Kingdom for a brochure. tel. +44 (0)1908 858785; fax +44 (0)1908 858787; e-mail ouwenq@open.ac.uk

The Open University
Walton Hall, Milton Keynes
MK7 6AA

First published 1997. Second edition 2005.

Edited and designed by The Open University.

Typeset by The Open University.

Printed and bound in the United Kingdom by Scotprint.

ISBN 0 7492 9664 X

2.1

31612B/a103b2i2.1

INTRODUCTION TO BLOCK 2

Written for the course team by Paula James and Janet Huskinson

In Block 2 you will be able to practise the skills you acquired while working on Block 1. Block 2 also marks a further step forward in your progress as a student of the humanities, for you will be asked to use these skills in order to approach a particular topic, the Colosseum and its role in both ancient and modern culture. In particular, you will be able to develop your techniques of close reading, close looking and close reasoning. As you work through the block you will experience the ways in which these techniques can all work together to help you tackle both straightforward and complex issues. You will, too, meet moral debate of a kind already familiar to you from Unit 4.

As well as building on familiar approaches, the next two weeks' work will introduce you to new areas of study. For example:

■ In Study Week 5 you will encounter the arts and social environment of the Romans, a society far removed from our own in time but nevertheless linked to the cultural environment in modern Europe. (Think of Roman roads such as the Fosse Way, of surviving physical features such as Hadrian's Wall and excavated sites of Roman villas, as well as words in English that derive from Latin, for example 'canine' from *canis*, dog.)

■ In order to study what happened in Roman times you will be asked to think about how historians work nowadays, how they find out about the past, what kinds of problem they encounter, how they present their judgements.

■ In Study Week 6 you will be introduced to the history of architecture, which has an important role in enabling us to relate past and present and to study ways in which buildings dating from different times may show significant differences as well as continuities in design and function.

Pacing your work

AGSG, ch.1, sect.4, 'Getting yourself organized' and ch.2, sects 3.3 and 3.4, 'Study sessions' and 'Setting targets'

As the course progresses you will be expected to take greater responsibility for organizing your time. (You will find it useful to consult *The Arts Good Study Guide* for advice on this.) To help you, we have divided the work in Unit 5 into six sections. Each section is designed to take about one and a half hours, leaving you time during the week to watch the associated television programme and to prepare material for your next TMA. Each section builds on aspects of what you have already studied and also introduces something new. This may be new information or concepts or a combination of both. It is important that you take time in each of your study sessions to digest the new material before you go on to the next. By the time you reach Study Week 6 you will be more experienced in organizing your work and will be aware of any kinds of study activity for which you feel you should allow more time. Unit 6 has longer sections and will contain more general guidance on appropriate places to take a break from study. In Study Week 6, to help you with architectural analysis, you will find a plan-reading exercise that should take roughly an evening's work. This has been written in such a way that you can if you wish bring it forward into Study Week 5 and spread your work in Unit 5 into the next week.

The block raises plenty of controversial questions, which we hope you will enjoy debating in your Study Centre group. You will also have the opportunity at summer school to explore some of these issues in more detail.

UNIT 5
THE COLOSSEUM

Written for the course team by Paula James and Janet Huskinson

Contents

STUDY COMPONENTS				
Weeks of study	Texts	TV	AC	Set books
1	*Illustration Book* *Resource Book 1*	TV5	AC3, Bands 1 and 2	–

Aims and objectives

The aims of this unit are:

1   to introduce you to the Roman world through a preliminary study of one of its most enduring symbols, the Colosseum (the Flavian Amphitheatre);

2   to encourage you to explore the form and the function of the building in its historical context;

and, in conjunction with Unit 6:

3   through an interdisciplinary case study, to develop the skills that you have acquired in Block 1 of close looking, close reading and close reasoning;

4   to demonstrate to you the advantages of an interdisciplinary approach to a historical period of lasting cultural significance.

By the end of this unit you should be able:

1   to distinguish between some main genres in ancient literature and art: for example, a letter, a poem, a biography, a mosaic, a coin, an inscription;

2   to make intelligent first moves in historical methodology: for example, evaluating source material and placing different types of evidence in context;

3   to start integrating the approaches of several humanities disciplines in order to gain a clearer picture of a given cultural artefact;

4   to examine critically how we receive and understand written and visual texts from the past and on what basis we make our assumptions and judgements about foreign cultures;

5   on a conceptual level, to identify some of the main challenges that a serious study of aspects of the Roman world presents.

Study note: using *Resource Book 1*

Section C in *Resource Book 1* contains texts that relate specifically to your study of the Colosseum in Block 2 and on AC3. Read through the Introduction to Section C in *Resource Book 1* now. This discusses the rationale behind the selection and ordering of the texts. It also provides some historical background to the period as a basis for your study.

1 INTRODUCTION

During your work on this unit you will discover that studying the Colosseum involves far more than looking at the building itself. We shall start by considering the Colosseum as a symbol of Roman culture, and then look at its depiction over the centuries and try to identify your own image of it. We shall then discuss its function, which we will consider in terms of two aspects: first, what the building was used for and how this determined its design, and second, the role of the building and the activities associated with it in the broader context of Roman social and political life.

Why the Colosseum?

Like Big Ben in London and the Eiffel Tower in Paris, the Colosseum in Rome is a large and distinctive element in the cityscape (as you can see from TV5, *The Emperor's Gift: the Colosseum* and Colour Plate 15, view across present-day arena). However, unlike these other monuments, the Colosseum is an ancient building. This makes it a natural symbol of the long history of Rome, the 'Eternal City'. In fact, the Colosseum is one of the most imposing buildings to survive anywhere in the Roman Empire (Figure 5.1).

It is also particularly 'Roman' in that it was built to house spectacular performances, which were an integral part of ancient Roman culture. Its size, antiquity and central place in ancient culture make it an obvious choice as the city's symbol. (A symbol is a visible sign that suggests or stands for an idea or concept. It is a term you met in Block 1, when looking at pictures. You should make sure that you are familiar with its use.)

In addition to these straightforward facts about the Colosseum, there are various stories that have come to be told about the building, which may strengthen its power as a symbol. The origins of the name 'Colosseum' are lost in obscurity, although this has been used as a nickname at least since the eighth century CE. One theory links the name to the massive size of the building; another derives it from the huge statue of the Emperor Nero, the Colossus, which stood close by. The word 'Colosseum' is sometimes translated into English as 'Coliseum', but the monument is properly known as the 'Flavian Amphitheatre', as the emperors who built it were from the Flavian family and 'amphitheatre' refers to the type of theatre where the seating runs all the way round.

(CE stands for Common Era. This means the current era, common to all cultures. With its counterpart BCE, Before the Common Era, it is used as

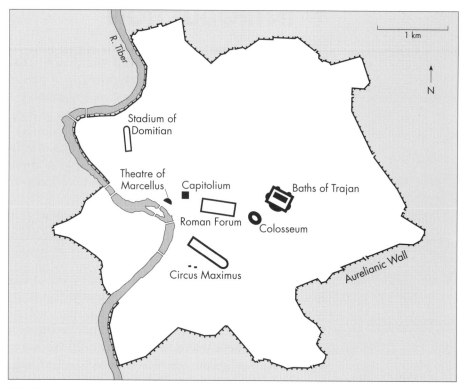

FIGURE 5.1 *Plan of ancient Rome showing the Colosseum in its historic context*

an alternative to AD and BC by many historians of the ancient world. You are likely to meet both forms of usage in your reading generally but CE/BCE are used in the course materials. Note that years and centuries BCE are counted backwards from the start of the Common Era: for example, the second century BCE is earlier than the first; the year 89 BCE is later than 90.)

The tales of what went on in the building have subsequently contributed to its almost legendary status. The ancient shows (often described as 'games') that it was built to house included gladiator fights, wild-beast displays and events in which condemned criminals and, later, Christians were put to death. These must have been dramatic enough at the time and they have certainly provided thrills in many modern books and films about ancient Rome. Dramas of deadly games played for real with full supporting cast of omnipotent emperors, bloodied gladiators, martyred virgins and hungry lions exert a fascination that somehow adds to the status of the Colosseum as a building of symbolism.

Yet they are horrific and they lead us to an obvious question. If these were the activities that it housed, why is the Colosseum still regarded as a symbol of Rome's glory? Degradation and shame might be what many people now may think more appropriate, whatever the grandeur and antiquity of the ruins.

AGSG, ch.2, sect.2.5, 'Points of view'

Here, it seems, there must be a clash of value judgements. Much of this unit will be looking at the place of the games in ancient Roman society and the values that were attached to them. Before you move on to this, it is important to consider how the Colosseum has reached us, at the cusp of the twentieth and twenty-first centuries, as a positive symbol of Rome's past. This will guide you towards identifying your own starting-point among the different judgements and expectations about its value.

How has the Colosseum been used as a symbol?

The Colosseum has been mentioned and depicted so often in literature and the visual arts that we can trace back its use as a symbol. The examples that follow show a range of ways in which it has been used, which shift slightly over time. Underpinning them all, however, is the idea that the Colosseum embodies the enduring greatness of the city of Rome. Even in the eighth century CE this was the view, to judge by the saying attributed to the English ecclesiastical writer, Bede:

> While stands the Coliseum, Rome shall stand
> When falls the Coliseum, Rome shall fall,
> And when Rome falls – the world.

Thus, the fate of the building was closely linked with the fate of the world itself.

EXERCISE

To obtain some sense of how responses to the Colosseum have changed, look closely at Plates 24–27 in the *Illustration Book*, which are typical of the way in which the Colosseum has been depicted in art from the twentieth back to the eighteenth centuries.

The modern strip cartoon in Plate 24 comes from a book in the famous Asterix series. The action is set in ancient Rome. The Colosseum provides the ultimate setting for drama and showdown as Asterix and his fellow Gauls tussle yet again with Roman authority. The cartoon gives an arena-level view of the mock-heroics. (It will be worth storing away in your mind some of the details depicted – armour, seating arrangements, etc. – to see how they compare with the reality, which you will see later in this week's work and in TV5.)

Plate 25 (Jean-Léon Gérôme, *Pollice verso*) shows another interior view of the Colosseum, set in ancient Rome. It is one of a number of large pictures which this artist painted of events in the amphitheatre and evokes the drama of an imagined event in history. There is the excitement of the critical moment, expressed in the Latin phrase of the title (the English translation is 'thumbs down'): will the emperor turn his thumb up or down – to signal life or death to the gladiator? Notice how the picture is packed with people and careful architectural detail.

Late nineteenth-century paintings like this inspired the settings of several early films which included amphitheatre scenes (for example, Enrico Guazzoni's *Quo Vadis* of 1912, which is discussed in TV7, *Passing Judgement*).

Plate 26 (C.W. Eckersberg, *The Interior of the Colosseum, Rome*) depicts a picturesque view inside the Colosseum; note how the arches are overhung with plants. You can see the Christian chapel at the centre, and the small shrines of the **Stations of the Cross**, which were erected around the arena (then still unexcavated) by Pope Benedict, who dedicated the building in 1749 to the early Christians martyred there. The old man praying is perhaps the Colosseum's resident hermit, recorded by the German writer Johann von Goethe in his *Italian Journey* (1787).

In the eighteenth century, a visit to Rome was an essential part of the '**Grand Tour**'. Those who made the tour were often portrayed in art with classical sights in the background as if to display their own aristocratic tastes. The couple in Plate 27 (John Singleton Copley, *Mr and Mrs Ralph Izard*) are shown with treasures of Greek and Roman art (like a still-life) and, set in the centre background, the Colosseum.

You will find it useful to think back to your work in Block 1 on looking at pictures, 'reading' their mood and composition, but in each of these examples concentrate on the building itself. Notice in particular the position it occupies, especially in relation to any people shown, and what it looks like. Is it, for instance, represented as a classical monument as yet undamaged, or as a picturesque ruin, or in some other form?

DISCUSSION

Did you notice that some of these pictures had ancient Rome for their setting whereas the others showed the Colosseum in the context of the time when they were painted? There is also a good deal of variety in their treatment of the subject. Even the ancient setting produced two rather different effects; these must reflect the artists' different purposes and not a change in the Colosseum itself! The nineteenth-century picture (Plate 25) aimed at dramatic realism, exploring the action, tensions and even the grandeur of the amphitheatre, whereas the cartoon (Plate 24) seemed more interested in the Colosseum as a 'typically Roman' backdrop for the exploits of the characters.

The other two pictures, set in more modern times, also use the Colosseum in different ways as a link with the past. In Plate 27 the figures seem to be looking appreciatively back at a classical past from their own present. The picture even suggests in their positions on either side of the ancient building that it is somehow central to their own relationship.

Plate 26 depicts a later Christian Colosseum, although it revels in the picturesqueness of the ancient ruins.

Plate 26 would appeal to the strong contemporary interest in 'romantic' Christian Rome and its sites and legends, which also found expression in literature. In the early nineteenth century, it seems, the sight of the Colosseum by moonlight was an experience craved by every fashionable visitor to Rome (Figure 5.2).

To sum up the exercise above, the four pictures show how, over just these two centuries, the significance of the Colosseum in relation to the main subjects of the scenes depicted is different. In addition, the scenes often relate to cultural interests of the particular times at which they were painted. (I could have used medieval and Renaissance examples too: see Plate 30, Maarten van Heemskerck, *Self-portrait with the Colosseum*.) On one hand, the building represents something enduring and unchanging, yet on the other, it seems to be open as a symbol to whatever different people may bring to it.

This leads us to consider the third and final question acting as a framework for this section.

What is your view of the Colosseum?

This is the point at which to stop for a minute to check your own response to the Colosseum and to note how it came about.

The reason for doing this is probably now clear: if, as the pictures we have considered have shown, the value attached to the Colosseum by the artists depends on the interests of their own time as much as on its ancient value, we need to think about *our own* interests before we go on to ask questions about the Colosseum in ancient Roman society.

For most tourists today the Colosseum is first of all an 'ancient monument', a major attraction to visit, imposing in its size yet puzzling in its intricate remains. It is the backdrop to holiday photographs and videos. But because it is such a well-known building we all 'know' something about it, although, as you have seen, such ideas may stand to be challenged.

FIGURE 5.2   *Engraving after a drawing by J.P. Cockburn,* Moonlight View in the Upper Corridors of the Colosseum, *published in* Views of the Colosseum, Rome, *W.B. Cooke, London, 1841. Metropolitan Museum of Art, New York*

AGSG, ch.2,
sect.5, 'Making
notes'

EXERCISE

Pause for a moment to jot down how the Colosseum appears in *your* mind's eye. As ancient ruins, or as a functioning amphitheatre filled with people? Do you see it as essentially pagan, or as part of a Christian tradition which is still commemorated by the large cross that stands inside (see Colour Plate 15)? Or as something else?

Think too about where your view originated. In a film or book, perhaps, or in some school-work about 'The Romans'? Or from a visit to the Colosseum itself or to another Roman amphitheatre, possibly the one at Verona, or those at Arles or Nîmes in southern France, which are still used today for mass spectacles of different kinds (Plate 28, Production of Verdi's *Aida* in Verona amphitheatre). ■

By stopping to consider your own image of the Colosseum and how this came about, you have identified what you yourself bring to the work on the building and its place in ancient society that you are about to begin.

2 REDISCOVERING THE ROMAN COLOSSEUM

So far, you have been introduced to a range of images of the Colosseum, with examples spanning the centuries. In the conclusion to the first section, you were asked to summarize your responses to the building. Section 2 encourages you to move on from this personal standpoint and to engage in a broader investigation of the form and function of the Colosseum. You should by the end of Block 2 be beginning to think about the nature of a historical inquiry of this kind and how historians use and evaluate the available evidence on the Colosseum.

In Block 3, Units 8 and 9 you will be guided through history as a discipline and provided with the methodological 'tools of the trade'. As you study Block 2, you should start to develop a greater critical awareness of the past and to see how we reach conclusions about what happened in particular civilizations and at particular times. Consider this building, the Flavian Amphitheatre (the Colosseum), as a very sizeable and significant artefact. It is the subject of your first substantial 'case study', so how are you going to approach it?

I would like you at this point to think about the best way to begin a study of this kind. There are 'coffee table' books on the subject, which have a useful overview of both the amphitheatre and the society that produced it. The authors of these very accessible but sometimes sensationalist books – they can come across as illustrated horrors of the Roman world! – frequently use their sketches and surveys of what went on in the arena to sum up or even summon up Roman civilization for the reader. They tend to simplify as well as to sensationalize.

A good way to begin a study of the Roman Colosseum is to read a thoughtful and thought-provoking piece of modern scholarship on the subject, which is at the same time aimed at students recently introduced to courses in the ancient world and so does not expect a detailed background knowledge from its readers. Thomas Wiedemann has made a lifelong study of the societies of Greece and Rome. In an article written for the classics journal *Omnibus* (1991), he introduces his reader to a range of ancient sources: for example, mosaics, remains of ancient amphitheatres, inscriptions and written works, which have survived from the time. Wiedemann confronts the controversial issues that are bound to arise in such a study: for instance, the rationale behind the games and the part the Colosseum and its arena played in Roman society – in short, what the Colosseum says about Roman civilization.

In reading and responding to Wiedemann, we have to come to grips with the challenge of what is involved in modern scholarship on the games. This means that we need to think not just about the available surviving evidence on the amphitheatres and what went on in them, but also about how such evidence might be represented and interpreted for the 'lay' reader.

EXERCISE

The *Omnibus* article by Wiedemann is reproduced in *Resource Book 1*, C11. Read this through quickly now and give some thought to the issues it raises. I hope that the points made in the introduction to this week's study will be illustrated and reinforced for you as you work through the article. You may remember, for instance, that you were asked to keep in mind both the simple function of the Colosseum as a place to house the games and the more complex issue of its role in a social and political context. Wiedemann's article focuses on the games rather than the cultural significance of the buildings provided for them, but you should also be thinking about this aspect of the Colosseum's function in Roman society as you read through the piece.

EXERCISE

AGSG, ch.2, sects.2 and 5, 'Your reactions to reading' and 'Making notes'

I would now like you to reread the *Omnibus* article, paying close attention to the way the whole article is organized. Try to summarize its sections, beginning with the issues the author raises in his opening two paragraphs. Do not fall into the trap of rewriting or paraphrasing the article at length. Just jot down what emerges as a main thread in each section. Remember, you can always refer to the relevant sections of *The Arts Good Study Guide* on reading and note-taking if you feel you need help on these topics.

DISCUSSION

Wiedemann's opening sentence may have had a familiar ring to you. He immediately raises the question of making judgements: what were the good and bad sides of Roman society? He is only too aware of the problem of repulsion when the full agenda of the games comes to light. What went on in the arenas is totally at variance with certain modern ideals (but not necessarily modern practice!) about the balance of nature and animal rights, the ethics of capital punishment and the persecution and martyrdom of those with a religious faith. Issues such as euthanasia and the treatment of animals have already appeared in the course (while identifying and following through positions in philosophical argument in Block 1). These are matters of considerable social significance and feelings about them run high in individuals, pressure groups and political parties.

Romans and Greeks

Wiedemann covers a lot of ground here. He gives a context for the Colosseum as a building that provided excellent facilities for the games, but he implies that even before this elaborate structure existed emperors were expected to put on entertainments for the people. The games became permanent fixtures for cities across the empire and were extremely popular even in Greece, the place that had given birth to a sophisticated culture several hundred years before Roman expansion. He does suggest that Greek and Roman philosophers (and later on, Christian thinkers) found the spectacles distasteful and harmful to the characters of the spectators.

The struggle with nature

This section could be subtitled 'Keeping law and order'. The emperor expected the gratitude of peoples throughout the empire for clearing cultivatable land of dangerous animals. This image of the ruler is a heroic one, demonstrating his power and benevolence. The figure of Hercules was a useful symbol for a number of emperors because in legend he had destroyed monsters over a wide geographical area, freeing communities of fear and allowing great cities to rise up out of them. (The bust of the Emperor Commodus as Hercules is shown in Plate 29. Colour Plate 16 shows how popular the image of the wild beast hunts became in art.)

You may have noted the points about the Colosseum being, initially, a monument to the Roman victory over the Jews who had rebelled against their Roman rulers in Judaea and, at the same time, a gift for the citizens of Rome to enjoy. Symmachus, a senator of Rome in the fourth century CE, complained bitterly about thirty Saxon pirates who robbed the Roman people of a fighting spectacle in the games he had organized. These prisoners of war strangled each other in their cells to avoid public death in the arena. In all respects, then, the Roman people were encouraged to identify with their rulers, to be associated with their supremacy and to support the suppression of all threats and opponents to the empire.

Life and death

Wiedemann deals briefly with the possible origins of the gladiatorial combats and lists the various ways of dealing death to condemned criminals in the arena. He suggests an ambivalence then as well as now in the matter of capital punishment. Public executions can be regarded as a remnant of less civilized times but they still happen in the world today. If we feel the phenomenon reveals ways of thinking about pain and death that are alien to us, it can be useful to think of the past as a foreign country where they do things differently.

For instance, Wiedemann suggests that the concept of collective responsibility for punishment in ancient Rome extended to the actual carrying out and witnessing of that punishment. Equally, the decision to pardon brave and successful fighters was a collective and popular one, according to Wiedemann. You may not have considered the amphitheatre as an icon or cultural symbol of the politics of participation! The implication is that a place like the Colosseum could provide an opportunity for a lively exchange between emperor and people, a kind of mutual manipulation in a public arena. At the same time, it could be argued that the spectators of the games gained a sense of social solidarity as citizens, reinforced by the 'otherness' of the unfortunate victims who performed before them.

Gentlemen and players

The supply and status of gladiators is the subject-matter of Wiedemann's final section. The chief source for the gladiator schools were the enslaved, enemies captured in war or revolt or those convicted of serious crime, men without any rights and totally at the mercy of their trainer at all times. There were also professional gladiators and it was possible to acquire charisma and become a star, supposedly fuelling the fantasies of women from all classes. The Emperor Commodus actually performed in the Colosseum. The Empress Faustina (his mother and wife of Marcus Aurelius), was allegedly smitten with the muscle men of the arena and it was rumoured that Commodus was the son of a gladiator. The ancient historians often included such anecdotes about the imperial household. Erotic obsessions with performers could affect emperors as well as empresses, but in this male-dominated society it was assumed that women were more readily led by their passions.

Wiedemann cites the martyrdom of St Felicity to illustrate a different kind of cult role for the gladiator. He suggests that for the Christian the gladiator could appear as a satanic adversary whose defeat would be the triumph of true faith over pagan ritual. Death in the arena could be welcomed as a test of courage for the Christians with the gladiator an agent of their glorious martyrdom. The strongly symbolic presence of the gladiator in the dreams of the imprisoned martyrs became a traditional feature of North African hagiographical writing (works by or about the saints).

High-born men might turn to the profession and their appearance in the arena tended to highlight the ambiguous attitudes towards the gladiators, who were both degraded beings outside society and glamorous attractions at the centre of it. Plates 31–34 show examples of mosaics featuring a variety of gladiator combats and Plate 35 shows a sculpted relief from Tomis in Romania. The frequency of these pictorial representations demonstrates the prevalence and popularity of the fighting figure of the arena. Figure 5.3 shows the tombstone of a gladiator.

I shall take a closer, more critical look at the assumptions about the community's reactions to the games in Section 3, when I evaluate Wiedemann's sources.

Wiedemann should have given you a lot to think about. His article takes us beyond horror at gratuitous violence and wholesale slaughter and encourages us to think about the arena as a place of punitive control and a statement of social identity. He spells out its relationship to the continuation of Roman power throughout the world and the exploitation of its form and function by the emperors to enhance their glory and emphasize their patronage of all citizens. He has gone part of the way towards explaining ancient attitudes to those who suffered at the games for the entertainment of the people. In order to draw his conclusions, he has collated a wide range of evidence from the ancient sources (the *Omnibus* article has just a few key examples) and attempted to reconstruct not just events but the consensus of the time about the games and their function.

In Section 3 you will be able to take a closer look at the ancient evidence (written and visual material dating from the Roman Empire) and review how modern scholars use these primary sources. (Primary sources are sources of

FIGURE 5.3 *Tombstone of gladiator Q. Vettius Gracilis, found at Nîmes. Musée archéologique de Nîmes*

information contemporary with a particular historical period. These may include written comments and descriptions as well as visual representations dating from the period. Secondary sources are comments on the period, or on sources contemporary with it, produced by modern authors.)

In Section 5, after you have had a chance to work through Band 1 of the audio-cassette on the Colosseum, I shall return to the question of judgements raised by Wiedemann's article and begin to integrate modern reactions with those of the ancient world. In other words, during the course of this study, you will be asked to think more deeply about responses ancient and modern to the spectacle of slaughter in the Colosseum. In Section 6 you will learn about the layout of the Colosseum. It should become clear from the evidence that the seating arrangements reflected the rigid hierarchy of Roman society, where everyone really did 'know their place'. This does not contradict Wiedemann's point about the gladiatorial games as 'ultimate democracy'; rather it suggests yet another aspect of the function of the amphitheatre. The Colosseum is a very good illustration not just of the elaborate structure needed to house large-scale games, but also of a place of unity and diversity – a potential flashpoint for all kinds of social tensions and shifting alliances between the different layers of society in attendance.

3 APPROACHING THE SOURCES

Wiedemann provides a broad survey of what went on in amphitheatres throughout the Roman Empire. He discusses the social implications of these activities, rather than merely describing them, so he covers the two aspects of the functions of the games (the content and context) suggested to you in the introduction to this unit. In order to reach his conclusions about these two aspects of the activities, he produces evidence from the ancient world itself.

Below is a brief summary of how Wiedemann might have approached and sifted the sources he uses. This summary should alert you to the basic methodology adopted by historians of the ancient world. You can certainly start asking some of these basic questions about any ancient historical source you encounter in your wider reading.

- First, Wiedemann would have identified the source and established its authenticity.

- Then he would have needed to put an accurate date to the source.

- The purpose for which the source was produced would obviously have been a key question. Establishing this would have involved both consideration of its form (a poem, a painting, an inscription) and the life and times of its producer.

- Finally, the strengths (contemporary comment) and weaknesses (possible exaggeration, bias, subjectivity) of the source would have been weighed up and reassessed in the context of other evidence from the period.

It is always possible that a source might be useful in furthering knowledge and understanding about another aspect of the society in question as well as or rather than the area under study.

Different types of written source

Graffiti

The piece of graffito (graffito is the singular of graffiti) referred to in Wiedemann's article reinforces the picture of the gladiator as a 'heart-throb'. Pompeii is a uniquely preserved ancient Italian city and very rich in personal and political slogans painted on walls. In Plate 36 (Graffiti outside House of Trebius Valens) there is an example of a painted advertisement for a show, which comes from a wall in Pompeii. The graffiti translate as:

> Dedication of the archives building by Cn. Alleius Nigidus Maius at Pompeii, 13 June: (there will be) a procession, a wild beast show, a display of athletes. The awning will be pulled across. Good luck to Nigra!

We shall be returning to the variety of archaeological and visual evidence this famous Italian town yields. Examples of its graffiti can be viewed in their original setting but are quite often reproduced in the form of written sources. One way of distinguishing these from a finished literary product, apart from seeing them as an informal and spontaneous activity, is to view such on-the-spot sloganizing or outpouring as an equivalent to 'oral history'. Not all of what you read in translation from Latin and Greek will have started out as words on a page.

Contemporary writings

In his *Omnibus* article, Wiedemann quotes from the Emperor Augustus' *Res gestae Divi Augusti* (*Achievements of the Divine Augustus*). This political testament took the form of a lengthy inscription, written by the emperor to be engraved upon the tomb of the imperial family, and deserves close attention for its mention of the games and their political implications. It has been dated to the year 14 CE, about sixty years before the Colosseum was built. Wiedemann uses these autobiographical writings of Augustus to highlight the importance of placating the people with lavish entertainments, that is, as evidence for the tradition of the games, although not for the Colosseum.

In its entirety the *Res gestae* looks like a fairly official and formal record of events in the reign of the Emperor Augustus, but it was written by the emperor himself and this is bound to alter our evaluation of it as a straightforward record. It was set up as a monument on bronze pillars outside his mausoleum in Rome. The inscription was intended to glorify his life and works for posterity, but as he wrote it in his lifetime it had a more immediate message and was designed to justify his unprecedented military and political power. Since it is propaganda, you should allow for a measure of exaggeration!

In a second allusion, Wiedemann draws upon the *Res gestae* as evidence for the large-scale slaughter of wild beasts and the fact that this was accepted, even celebrated. Perhaps you noted the usefulness of this source for both statistics (numbers of animals likely to be killed) and attitudes (what a powerful and generous leading citizen was expected to do for the Roman people on his own account).

Augustus is not likely to play down the numbers of those slaughtered for the entertainment of the people. He recites the lists in a matter-of-fact way, but he is clearly proud of the impressive displays. Even the 'trained' modern scholar can fall into the trap of accepting and repeating such boasts from the ancient sources uncritically. Although the modern reader may react to the catalogue of slaughter with dismay, Augustus expects a very different response from his audience, which raises the issue of how it was received at the time. Augustus implies that he was financing the events as well as putting them on. It is significant that Augustus kept the giving of the games very much in the imperial family. This should set you thinking about the function of the spectacles in the political life of Rome, how the staging of such shows increased the prestige, status and influence of those who financed and organized them.

Texts from the later empire

Two of the texts Wiedemann refers to in his *Omnibus* article have a distinctly Christian flavour: St Augustine's *Confessions* and the description of the martyrdom of St Felicity. The extract from St Augustine's *Confessions* is part of a moral and admonitory tale about a young man fallen into bad company and becoming 'hooked' on the euphoria of spectator sport. The full story appears in *Resource Book 1*, C10 and you will be asked to read this in Section 5. The displays of blood-letting could totally engage the emotions of the onlookers. The tone of the extract indicates the disapproval of the author, but that is really a side issue for Wiedemann. He has set out to prove how prevalent the popularity of the games must have been in places elsewhere than Rome, not to focus on dissenting voices on the games.

Of course, no one is able totally to ignore the preconceptions and the ways of thinking that their own society has helped to form, so we should not accept too uncritically the conclusions about the Colosseum we read by modern classical scholars. In Section 6 we shall read a short piece from another modern classical historian and use it as a brief contrast with Wiedemann's approach.

Different types of visual source

Buildings of the same type

As Wiedemann quotes from ancient authors, the editors of the journal *Omnibus* illustrated his article with appropriate pictures. Look back at the illustrations of the same subjects in *Resource Book 1*, C11.

The El Djem amphitheatre is featured as a fine example of one of the 'copycat' arenas discussed in the first section of Wiedemann's article. These provide us with several pieces of visual evidence, which, along with the many existing remains in other sites, emphasize the central importance of the games and the focal point of the arena in urban areas throughout the empire.

There are other inferences we can draw from a piece of archaeological evidence of this type. The amphitheatre at El Djem is a variation on the Colosseum design. The ambitious compass of the Colosseum proved a winning formula, elaborating upon a design that had already been used for arenas in Italy. It combined architectural grandeur with a successful structure for safety and crowd control. El Djem could also be seen as an example of the proliferation of Roman civic ideology and the Romanization of the provinces in general.

Decorative art

The mosaic from the Roman villa at Nennig is one of many examples available to us from a wide-ranging sample of surviving floor decorations. Gladiator scenes frequently appear upon them. The mosaic and the sculptured relief form part of the evidence for what went on in the actual combats. We also have literary descriptions of the varied skills, weapons and categories of the gladiatorial art.

Wiedemann has no room in his article and, indeed, it is not within its remit to go into detail about styles of fighting in the arena. So I would suggest that the illustrations decorate the text rather than clarify the activities in the arena touched upon by Wiedemann. The pictures do play upon the imagination of the reader and convey something of the atmosphere at the shows, although they are perhaps too stylized to give us a sense of movement or excitement.

One of the mosaics from El Djem appears in Plate 34 and the Nennig mosaic is reproduced in Plate 39. How to use the mosaic as a source is discussed in an exercise on AC3.

In conclusion, then, there are many ancient sources for the Colosseum; they are varied and often exciting to use for a study of the games and of the society of the games. There are also informed and informative books and articles dealing with the Colosseum as a historical phenomenon. Section C in *Resource Book 1* provides a further selection of both types of evidence.

4 CASSETTE EXERCISES

AGSG, ch.3, sect.3.2, 'Broadcasts and cassettes'

In this section your study is based on a different medium: the audio-cassette. The aim of this is to give you the opportunity of engaging with significant written and visual evidence from the Roman period and to give you further practice in exploring the kinds of question historians of the period are likely to ask when confronted with material like this. You will be able to hear samples of Latin verse followed by English translations and then you will be guided on how to approach visual sources. We hope you enjoy this change of focus, which will allow you a more personal interaction with the material and the course writers.

Written sources

In order to develop critical awareness you need some basic information about a source. Before you listen to AC 3, Side 1, Band 1, please read through the following introduction to Martial and his poetry.

Martial (40–103/104CE) was a Spanish provincial famous for his satirical epigrams (short poems written in elegiac couplets, a verse form also used for love poetry and lament). Martial wrote a book of epigrams, *Liber de spectaculis* (*The Book of Spectacles* or *Shows*), to celebrate the opening of the Colosseum in 80 CE. This may have been commissioned by the Emperor Titus, who presided over the inaugural games. The publication of the book marks the poet's emergence from obscurity. Eleven of Martial's poems are reproduced in translation in *Resource Book 1*, C1 and you may find it interesting to read them through to begin to appreciate the content and style of his work.

CASSETTE 3, SIDE 1, BAND 1

Listen to AC3, Side 1, Band 1 now. This focuses on three of the poems by Martial reproduced in *Resource Book 1*, C1: poems 3, 5 and 10. On the cassette the poems are read in Latin and in English, and transcripts are given below. (Note: you will notice some variation between my English translations of the poems given below and those of D.R. Shackleton Bailey reproduced in *Resource Book 1*.)

As you listen to his poems, you will need to bear in mind that Martial was expected to produce extravagant praise for the emperor and the entertainment this emperor has bestowed as a gift (*munus*) on the people of Rome. However, he was also showing off his poetic art, his skill with metre and his creative power to produce images and to convey the sense of excitement and anticipation at the miraculous sights in the arena. ■

Poem 3

Iunctam Pasiphaen Dictaeo credite tauro:
    vidimus. accepit fabula prisca fidem.
nec se miretur, Caesar, longaeva vetustas:
    quidquid Fama canit, praestat harena tibi.

It's true! Pasiphae did mate with the Cretan bull.
We've seen it done. The old legend is proved.
The past needn't preen itself, however antique.
Whatever story Fame tells us, the arena puts it on show.
And for you, Caesar!

Poem 5

Prostratum vasta Nemees in valle leonem
    nobilis Herculeum Fama canebat opus.
prisca fides taceat: nam post tua munera, Caesar,
    haec iam feminea vidimus acta manu.

Celebrated Tradition has been in the habit of singing of the lion felled in the vast valley of Nemea, a labour of Hercules.
Time for 'true tales of the past' to be quiet; for, after your shows, Caesar, we have
witnessed deeds like this here and how, and one by a woman's hand!

Poem 10

Lambere securi dextram consueta magistri
    tigris, ab Hyrcano gloria rara iugo,
saeva ferum rabido laceravit dente leonem:
    res nova, non ullis cognita temporibus.
ausa est tale nihil, silvis dum vixit in altis:
    postquam inter nos est, plus feritatis habet.

A tigress, rare glory from the Caspian mountains, trained to lick her master's right hand, savagely ripped a wild lion apart with her ferocious teeth.
An unprecedented event! never heard of before.
She did not dare do such a deed while she lived in the depths of the forest.
After being among us, she has acquired more savagery.

Poem 3 refers to what seems to have been a particularly gross spectacle involving a condemned female prisoner coerced into copulation with a bull. It is interesting that the second century CE author and orator Apuleius describes arrangements for a similar punishment in his novel *The Golden Ass* (see the extract in *Resource Book 1*, C2). The ass (who is in fact the bewitched human hero) manages to escape before the entertainment commences, so he avoids what, ironically, he regards as a humiliation *for him* in copulating with a criminal.

The mention by Martial of female gladiators (poem 5) demonstrates yet another bizarre role for women in the arena. In poem 4, Martial makes a mythological inference by introducing the idea of Venus, Roman goddess of love, serving Caesar (Titus), which is a pretty compliment to the reigning emperor. Venus was also a fostering figure for the city of Rome because her son, Aeneas, the exiled prince of Troy, was popularly believed to be the founding father of the early Roman settlement. The combination of Venus with Mars (Roman god of war but, like Venus, regarded as a special patron and ancestor of the Romans) brings in yet another subtext. Mars and Venus had indulged in a famous affair, been caught in the act and publicly humiliated. (The Greek version of the scandal can be found in Homer's *Odyssey*.) It was a standard device to talk about sexual activity in terms of military combat, but Martial also clearly enjoys making mythical innuendos out of the spectacle of the woman gladiator. Female gladiators are shown in Plate 37.

The third poem you hear on the cassette (poem 10) focuses on the tigress from a far-flung land. It was expected that the shows would include an exotic array of dangerous animals to impress the spectators. (You might recall Wiedemann at this point, as he explores some of the motivations underlying wholesale destruction of species.) In *Resource Book 1* you will find another relevant extract from Apuleius (C3). The story of Demochares and his bears illustrates the hazards of capturing and housing such animals safely and without expensive losses! See also the letter from Pliny the Younger, which refers to the same subject (C4). A relief showing a transport ship appears in Plate 38 and Section 6 will also refer to the collection and keeping of the animals.

For the present, let us just note that the exultation and voyeurism the Martial poems convey to us, the modern reader, very probably served more than one purpose for the poet himself. There is, in the first place, fulsome praise of the emperor, who takes on semi-divine status by staging such wondrous sights. The suggestion that he brings alive and somehow validates the truth of well-worn myths is surely part of the panegyric (poem of praise). It may be 'tongue in cheek', but the tradition of such poetry was to make extravagantly 'over-the-top' claims for one's patron.

We can assume that Martial is also working through his own agenda. He has a literary artist's interest in transferring visual excitement into the medium of poetry, for his own lasting fame. He shows a preoccupation with clever acts of fortune and he likes to stress the paradox and ingenuity of events in the arena. The strange sights, whether the participants are human or animal, have been captured for posterity and 'performances' at the games are recreated on the page.

It must, too, have been particularly fascinating for a poet well versed in all the traditions and material of his craft to witness what he interprets as the visualization of famous myths. The stories of Greek and Roman myth and legend had been recycled by the poets for centuries. Hence Martial's exuberant depiction of punishments which, for us, are excessively and bizarrely cruel, the sorts of scene we would expect to witness through the medium of cinema, in rough-justice shocker films of the 1990s. The issue of voyeurism will be explored in TV7.

Visual sources

CASSETTE 3, SIDE 1, BAND 2

Listen to AC 3, Side 1, Band 2 now. This contains exercises to help you consider the types of question you will need to ask to reveal the evidence provided by a visual source. The two examples given specifically relate to your study of the Colosseum and the games. I have chosen examples that more or less correspond in type to those used by the editors of the journal *Omnibus* to illustrate Wiedemann's article: relief decoration (but here in a very different form, not a sculpture but a coin) and floor mosaic. You will have some familiarity with these through your work on them in Section 3. (The third type used by Wiedemann is a building, and the opportunity to study the Colosseum as a building will come in TV5, and with an exercise on interpreting plans in Unit 6.) You will need to study Colour Plate 14 (Sestertius of Titus) and Plate 39 (Scenes from the arena, floor mosaic) while listening to the cassette. ■

The first example is a bronze Roman coin (a sestertius) from 80 CE showing on one side the Emperor Titus (Titus Vespasianus Caesar) and on the other a representation of the Colosseum.

General questions you might ask about this source are:

■ How old is it?

■ What is it made of?

■ Where did it come from?

■ What is its value, ancient and modern?

■ What is the significance of its decoration?

However, you should also be aware of the importance of the *purpose* of a source in indicating its potential value as evidence. The *content* of a source may provide evidence not only as a literal interpretation but also as a record of the significance of an event. The decoration of the coin celebrates the impact made by the inauguration of the Colosseum, reflecting imperial pride, rather than accurately depicting the building itself.

The second example is an early third century CE floor mosaic from a Roman villa at Nennig in Germany.

You are asked to consider the possibilities and limitations of this source as a potential form of evidence for the Colosseum and the games.

Where do its possibilities lie?

- Its location (both its domestic setting and its occurrence in a province of Rome) shows the widespread popularity of the games.

- It documents some activities that do not survive: for example, types of gladiator, animal combat, etc. (However, these do pose the question of realism: see below.)

- It evokes the atmosphere of drama, smells, noise and bloodshed of the games.

What are its possible limitations?

- As decorative art, its prime function was to decorate a floor rather than document the games.

- As an art form, mosaic tended to repeat standard *generic* scenes rather than original compositions. Scenes cannot be taken as sources of accurate evidence for historical details. Look at Plates 40 and 41 (Helmet and Parade armour) for comparison. In addition, it is not clear how much say an individual patron would have had in the choice of motifs.

In summary, when estimating the value of a source as evidence, we need to consider: the purpose of the source; its content; the artistic conventions used; and the roles of different people in creating it. The source can then be used in conjunction with other sources to provide *comparative* evidence or to further our knowledge as *supplementary* evidence.

5 JUDGEMENTS: ANCIENT AND MODERN PERCEPTIONS OF THE GAMES

AGSG, ch.5, sect.5.2, 'Using evidence'

In his article in the journal *Omnibus*, Wiedemann raised the issue of repulsion. You have had a chance to evaluate both the context and the function of the Colosseum and to hear, through the poems of Martial, how punitive power was exercised in the arena. You have seen how evidence about the games and the arenas can be derived from great ruins as well as small coins. I would now like you to consider the question of reactions, ancient and modern, to the building and the entertainments it came to represent.

Modern reactions

EXERCISE

Please read *Resource Book 1*, C12 for an uncompromising condemnation of the games from a classical scholar of this century. The extract is from John Pearson's *Arena: the story of the Colosseum* (1973). It would be useful to compare and contrast his approach with Wiedemann's.

- How does Pearson begin his description and what sort of tone does this lend to the passage?

- Contrast this with Wiedemann's opening observations. They may be covering similar ground but how are they framing the issues?

DISCUSSION

You probably picked up the immediately judgemental air of the 'most disgusting, organized mass binge' in the Pearson extract. Wiedemann also identified the repulsion most people would feel on learning about the slaughter in the arena, but he moved fairly rapidly on to suggest a historical context for our reactions today as well as for the beliefs and customs of the ancient Romans.

It is possible to identify a significant difference between Pearson and Wiedemann in Pearson's rather puzzled air when he writes of Titus: 'And yet this kindly man shared his father's passion for the arena.' In the first place, Pearson seems to assume that the ancient biographers and historians give reliable representations of the emperors (although their tendency to reproduce rumour and anecdote has been noted already). In the second place, the biographer Suetonius' picture of the generous Titus cites this very participation in and indulgence at the shows to demonstrate the goodness and kindness of the emperor (see *Resource*

Book 1, C5). This was clearly not a contradiction for the Romans, although Pearson is not wrong to identify it as a problem for scholars and students of the ancient world.

The phenomenon of the games and their popularity does demand the sort of discussion entered into by Wiedemann about the Roman mind set. Pearson's 'this was a vulgar age' does not really answer fundamental questions about the psychology of spectacle or the concept of social control in all its manifestations.

On the other hand, you might have felt a sense of relief that Pearson does not sanitize the 'most disgusting, organized mass binge' of the inaugural games. Wiedemann is not totally dispassionate about ancient custom and tradition but he is matter-of-fact about ways of dealing out punishment and about the principles behind public executions and cleansing the community of criminals.

If you want to read more on this subject, there is a book on the games by R. Auguet, published in translation as *Cruelty and Civilisation* (1972), which suggests the tensions the modern reader perceives between the crude entertainments and high artistic and intellectual achievements this one society contained.

Moving back to the ancient evidence

It is important, of course, to differentiate between the experience and attitudes of the ancient world and the material and spiritual conditions of our own times. However, it is possible, when drawing this essential distinction, to impose a uniformity on Roman society that did not necessarily exist and to assume that there were no dissenting voices who spoke against the spectacles. In other words, ask yourself how far we can generalize about Roman responses to the games.

You might expect the educated men, the philosophers and thinkers, to find the tastes of the mob unpalatable, whatever these might be. This is largely true, but the cultural divide in the ancient world is not necessarily straightforward. Indicating contempt for entertainments enjoyed by the masses is one way of elevating one's own taste and status and claiming to have a monopoly on finer feelings.

It is the educated élite who were able to articulate their attitudes towards the games in a coherent and written form. We can see this in a piece of ancient evidence from Cicero, a famous lawyer, orator and politician living in the turbulent times of the late Roman Republic: see *Resource Book 1*, C6, an extract from one of Cicero's letters, written about 100 years before the building of the Colosseum. Many of Cicero's 900 letters were clearly intended for publication and his eleven books of correspondence can read like an organized history of the time. Cicero prided himself on taking an educated interest in human behaviour. His letter about the audience's reaction to Pompey's elephants is of interest because it acknowledges that the mob could feel compassion towards suffering animals. (This incident is discussed in TV7.) Also in *Resource Book 1* is an extract from a poem by Statius (C7), in which a noble and courageous lion has human feelings and motivations ascribed to it.

The beginning of Cicero's letter suggests that there were contrary opinions about the games, even at a time when they were wildly popular. In another letter (see *Resource Book 1*, C8), Cicero expressed his feeling that the combats and the courage shown at the games were object lessons in good old Roman virtues, the strength and stamina that had made the city great. This opinion was shared by another prolific letter writer, Pliny the Younger. Pliny too, writing in the era of the Colosseum, underlined the importance of displays of skill and bravery.

Both Pliny and Cicero recognized the role the games played in gaining prestige and status for those in political life (see *Resource Book 1*, C4). Such shows were seen as essential 'networking' for this very purpose, impressing one's peers and the populace at large in all parts of the empire. The gladiator contest seems to have originated as ostentatious display at aristocratic funerals, where slaves and prisoners of war fought to the death in honour of the deceased. In a sense its function did not so much change as expand and serve a more complex political purpose over time. The mosaic shown in Colour Plate 17 ('Magerius') is a good example of this. In the centre stands a boy holding a tray of money bags. The long inscriptions on either side of him are meant to represent the shouts exchanged between the herald who acts as 'ring-master' to the show and the audience. Essentially they urge Magerius, the show's financial backer, to make generous payment to the firm which provided the show: the money bags show how well he responded. To make the situation even more imposing, two gods – Dionysus and Diana – are shown as onlookers.

In contrast, we find clearly expressed qualms that the combats could degenerate into crude blood-letting. The philosopher Seneca, who virtually ruled Rome for five years on behalf of the young Emperor Nero, saw few redeeming features in the lunch-time entertainments the arena provided. (Note: this is still in an era predating the Colosseum – Nero saved himself from execution by committing suicide in 68 CE.)

EXERCISE

Read the letter from Seneca reproduced in *Resource Book 1*, C9. Then read the extract from St Augustine's *Confessions* in *Resource Book 1*, C10. The objections to the games of the Christian writer St Augustine were alluded to by Wiedemann. Can you identify any similarities in attitude between the two ancient writers?

DISCUSSION

Seneca gives the reader a lesson in group dynamics. He had attended the games at midday to watch a varied programme of gladiatorial skills. Instead he witnessed sheer butchery and a mockery of the kind of courageous combat Cicero may have had in mind when he put the case for fighting spectacles. Seneca is primarily concerned, as is Augustine, with its effects on the audience.

Augustine monitors the corruption of Alypius from his first sight of the games and describes how they assail the senses and sensibilities of the onlookers. He believes that the constant arousal of violent passions is damaging for the soul and spirituality of the spectator. Although Seneca talks more in philosophical terms about the destruction of rationality and the submission to baser instincts, he too describes the addictive effects of death and suffering as spectator sports.

If you were expecting the Christian voice to introduce ideas of mercy and the sanctity of human life, that is, to focus on the victims of the arena, then you would have looked in vain. Neither Seneca, who had his human and sensitive side, nor St Augustine, a Christian bishop, reveals a great deal of anxiety about the custom of public punishment from the point of view of the victims who suffered it.

The Christian polemicist Tertullian, writing in North Africa in the second century CE, attempted to discourage the faithful from attendance by focusing on the resonances of old rituals which surrounded the games and which accentuated their pagan origins and atmosphere. It would seem, then, that the entertainments offered in the amphitheatres attracted people of all beliefs, including Christians, even at a time when Christians were themselves subject to persecution.

In fact, in spite of the manifold suffering of Christians in the arena, especially and most frequently in the provincial amphitheatres, a Christian like Tertullian was capable of relishing the future punishment of the pagans on Judgement Day in the context of a public spectacle. However, actual games to the death were eventually systematically opposed by Christian bishops in a Christianized empire. The Emperor Honorius (393–423 CE) apparently banned them. However, the extracts from a book by Wiedemann, *Emperors and Gladiators* (1992), reproduced in *Resource Book 1*, C13, suggest that this was not the end of the story! (For a fifth century representation of an animal hunt in the arena, presided over by officials, see Figure 5.4.)

AGSG, ch.3, sect.2, 'Learning with other people'

This section should have given you plenty to think about and to discuss in tutorials or study groups. Justification for the games in their own time seems to have been based not just on ideas about fitting punishments for wrong-doers but also on assumptions about skilled combat as a 'noble art' which should be regularly displayed. Fighting skills were bound to be

FIGURE 5.4 *Ivory plaque with officials at a* venatio
[deer hunt in arena], ivory, early fifth century CE,
*29.4 x 12 x 0.6 cm. Liverpool Museum.
(Reproduced by permission of the Board of Trustees
of the National Museums and Galleries on
Merseyside)*

a preoccupation of a warlike and expansionist civilization with a high military profile.

Opposition to the games, as we have seen, focused on the undesirable effects upon the spectators. It is not unusual for modern arguments against capital punishment to express similar anxieties about the mental state of those who decide upon, consent to or have to carry out 'legalized murder'. Perhaps the reactions of ancient writers like Seneca and St Augustine are not too difficult to relate to modern perceptions of brutalization and psychological damage arising from violence perpetrated by an institution or state.

The general lack of concern among ancient writers for the suffering of the condemned (with the exception of the Christian martyrs who were innocent in the eyes of those who shared their faith) is more problematic. It is difficult not to superimpose the moral values of our own society upon the customs and codes of the Roman world. The occasional moments of compassion from the spectators reported by some of the contemporary writers perhaps only reinforce the difference between modern and ancient attitudes. Counterposed to these reports are graphic descriptions (both written and visual) of the wholesale slaughter of exotic animals and the painful deaths of the condemned. Ancient spectators were viewing gladiators as, in the main, hardened criminals condemned for terrible crimes (see the discussion in TV7).

The occasional dressing-up of the condemned as mythological characters, forcing them to re-enact famous scenes of death and suffering from legend, goes beyond normal concepts of just retribution. You heard how death became spectacle in this theatrical sense on the audio-cassette (Martial). An article by Kathleen Coleman in the *Journal of Roman Studies* (key selections from this are provided in *Resource Book 1*, C16) offers a cultural framework even for these extremes. Her comments are meant to be controversial and should stimulate tutorial discussion.

I hope that coming to a better understanding of Roman ethics and behaviour has involved a re-examination of your own assumptions about the way a society controls its citizens and behaves towards its 'criminals' and 'deviants'. Do you think it is ever possible for a civilization to make sanctity of human life an absolute principle?

This part of our case study has, by necessity, concentrated upon a very notorious and emotive aspect of Roman society. I hope, though, that you have developed a sufficiently broad historical perspective on the Colosseum to pursue a general study of this period in an informed and confident way in the future, if you choose to do so.

6   THE FORM OF THE BUILDING

You have now seen how the games in the Colosseum fitted into a long cultural tradition in Rome. Was there a comparable tradition for the building?

According to the poet Martial the Colosseum was highly exceptional. As you know from Section 4, his poems to celebrate its opening used elaborate imagery to compliment the emperor, so it is no surprise to find that he compares it favourably, and in high-flown terms, to the seven wonders of the ancient world (see *Resource Book 1*, C1, poem 1). For Martial at least, the Colosseum transcended even the most extraordinary building traditions.

This section will take a more measured look at the historical context of the building and then at how its design met the basic needs of spectators and spectacles. Many of these points are covered in closer detail in TV5, whilst next week's work in Unit 6 develops them in a different context, that of architectural history.

Amphitheatres

The word 'amphitheatre' comes from two Greek words which together literally mean 'a place with seats for spectators all round'. This points to a major difference in design between amphitheatres and other Greek and Roman theatres, where the seating did not completely enclose the space for performances. Romans also used the term 'arena' for the building, from the Latin *harena* for 'sand' which was used to cover the surface of the performing area. (In what follows 'arena' will be used only for the performing area.)

Even these names for the physical building-type suggest that it stands apart from the main Greek and Roman tradition of theatre design and was not directly inherited – as were many things Roman – from the Greek.

Pompeii

The case of Pompeii and its amphitheatre (Figure 5.5) is another good illustration of the cultural roots of the amphitheatre.

During the second century BCE Pompeii's prosperity had increased. Like many of its neighbours in the area surrounding modern Naples (an area then known as Campania) it shared in the predominantly Greek culture which was common to major cities around the Mediterranean. Commerce and travel had spread the taste for things Greek and stimulated the wealth for these towns to acquire them. So it was that many of the richer houses in Pompeii at this time were decorated with mosaics and wall-paintings that reflected the cosmopolitan Greek-based culture, whilst the town boasted a Greek-type theatre for its entertainment.

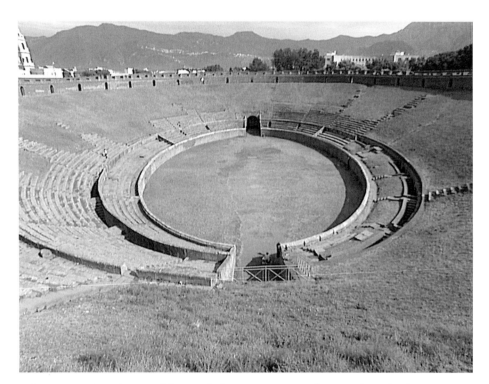

FIGURE 5.5   *Aerial view of the amphitheatre, Pompeii. (Photograph: Index/Pizzi)*

In 80 BCE there was a major change in the status of the town, which brought with it some telling developments in terms of public buildings. Pompeii was chosen for a settlement of Roman army veterans and given new civic status (see Figure 5.6). Various new buildings were erected to provide the town with facilities that would befit this role as a Roman centre. Among these was an amphitheatre that seated about 20,000 people. Here, then, is a clear sign that the amphitheatre was something that belonged with the Roman concept of a town – as is reflected too in the way in which amphitheatres were later built in cities founded or developed by the Romans throughout their empire.

The amphitheatre at Pompeii is also important in the history of these buildings, as it is the oldest permanent amphitheatre to survive. In the earliest days, gladiatorial combats were probably held outdoors in natural arenas, with spectators watching from the slopes of a convenient hillside; where this was impossible, temporary seating had to be constructed. Most often this would have been made of wood, which has long since perished. Colour Plate 18 shows a contemporary wall-painting of the amphitheatre at Pompeii.

FIGURE 5.6 *Map of Italy showing the relative positions of Rome and Pompeii*

Rome

Literary and archaeological evidence suggests that in Rome gladiatorial shows were held in the Forum, 'the political and cultural centre of the city', certainly in the late first century BCE. There are also some references in literature to amphitheatres built in the later first century BCE and earlier first century CE, but nothing survives even though one at least was allegedly built of stone (30 BCE). Some were burned down. One outside Rome collapsed, with considerable loss of life.

When, in 71 CE, the Emperor Vespasian started to build his great amphitheatre, the Colosseum, he made a popular move. He was giving to the people of Rome a huge, permanent setting for the gladiatorial shows, which would accommodate about 50,000 people. Even his choice of site was politically clever as it had been land appropriated by his predecessor Nero for a much resented palace. Martial, of course, wrote appreciatively of this (see *Resource Book 1*, C1, poem 2).

Work progressed fast. The first stages were dedicated in 75 CE and Vespasian's successor, Titus, was able to inaugurate the extended building in 80 CE. However, throughout its ancient history, as you can see from the list of important dates for the Colosseum in *Resource Book 1* (p.91), building and repair work were constantly under way (see, for example, the buttress in Plate 43).

The Colosseum and its functions

The rest of this section will consider how the Colosseum fulfilled its functions, but first you need to be clear about the basic features that its design needed to incorporate.

EXERCISE

Please stop for a moment to consider what would have been required, bearing in mind what you have already learned about the Colosseum and the activities that it housed.

DISCUSSION

My list would include sufficient space; visibility (especially for VIP guests, but a central part of this public spectacle was the interaction between performance and *all* the spectators); points of access into the ring; adequate barriers between the arena and the seating (not just for the people at the front against escaping performers but for everyone against crush and riots); and facilities for cleaning, drainage and disposal.

EXERCISE

How did the Colosseum provide for these needs?

Most obvious from pictures (Colour Plate 19, Colosseum, Rome, aerial view) and plans is the sheer size of the arena (3357 square metres/ 36,134.8 square feet), which gave space for many spectators and scope for various types of events and the provisions necessary to accommodate them. The complex structure of the building allowed excellent access and visibility and optimum safety for performers and spectators.

Let us look more closely at requirements for spectators and performers and how these were met.

Provision for spectators

Probably the most striking feature of the seating in the Colosseum, even today, is its sheer volume. It catered, it seems, for 45,000 spectators with perhaps 5000 more standing. To manage this, the construction had to be capable of bearing massive weights. This was achieved through the use of enormous piers to carry the arches and corridors and of different building materials for optimum effect. Although people seated in the uppermost tiers were in fact some distance away from the arena, the continuous rows of seating gave everyone an unobstructed view.

There was a good system of public access via seventy-six numbered entrances into the amphitheatre. Spectators entered by openings that presumably matched numbered tickets, climbed wide staircases to the appropriate landings (Plates 42(a) and (b), Corridors and landings), and thence went to their seats. Entrances on the short sides of the amphitheatre show traces of richer decoration, with stuccoed ceilings (Plate 44) and marble panelling. These led directly to the boxes overlooking the arena used by the emperor and his suite.

People need refreshment and shade. Water was provided for refreshment by a system of pipes, which fed fountains on the landings, and shade was created by a kind of vast sun-shade, which could be drawn across the arena. Its support must have been a major feat of engineering in itself, and a special unit of sailors was stationed nearby to work it, although how this was actually done is unclear. The projections that are visible on the upper levels of the building (Plate 45, points of attachment for sun-shade) were probably part of its arrangement.

However, there is one other factor governing seating arrangements in the Colosseum which is not obvious from the practical viewpoint. This relates to Roman social legislation, which allocated seating to spectators according to their particular social rank or personal status. This arrangement stressed the symbolic aspect of the occasion: a microcosm of Roman society witnessing an event that had a symbolic as well as entertainment content.

The chief figure in the audience (at times the chief performer) was, of course, the emperor. He needed to be at the centre of attention, and his actions had to be visible to the audience. His box was at the centre of one of the long sides of the amphitheatre. Opposite him on the other side sat dignitaries of the city, the consuls and the vestal virgins.

If we look at the seating as it survived in the building, these distinctions are visible in the five different sectors of seating separated by landings. At the lowest level would sit senators; then came the so-called *maenianum primum* (the first gallery), which comprised at least eight rows of marble seating; then the *maenianum secundum* (the second gallery), which was divided into upper and lower sections; and finally the *maenianum summum* (the uppermost gallery). This had rows of wooden seating for women and slaves.

Inscriptions carved on stairways and on the backs of seats – which now usually only survive in fragmentary form – designated the seating. Only for senators, who sat according to family groups, were seats reserved by name. As for safety measures, spectators in the front seats were separated from the arena by a balustrade, and archers were apparently stationed in the higher levels to shoot into the arena if trouble broke out.

Provision for the performers

Performers required sufficient space in the arena for their acts, appropriate accommodation, and entrances and exits. There also had to be work spaces for the service staff, who had to manage a fast 'turn-around' between events in the arena, often with a huge number of performers. The inaugural games given by the Emperor Titus in 80 CE are said to have lasted for 100 days and involved the slaughter of thousands of animals and fights of up to 3000 men in a single day. Some lavish animal displays required realistic landscaping to be put up. All this needed labour and organization to stage the shows and shift the bodies, living and dead.

These were the basic requirements, but they were met in different ways according to the needs and status of the particular performers. After all, a variety of events was staged in the Colosseum: a typical major day at the games began with beast shows, moved to the execution of criminals and prisoners and culminated in the gladiatorial combats. The gladiators were housed outside the Colosseum in barracks nearby (the *Ludus Magnus*, which even included a smaller training arena: see Plate 47), and made a ceremonial entry into the arena, but the beasts and prisoners had to brought into the building, held securely and somehow driven into the arena when their turn came.

The entrance for the gladiators, therefore, was wide and conspicuous, set on the main axis of the building. They paraded through it accompanied by officials and various musicians, and passed in front of the presiding authorities in their boxes before fighting in various types of combat. The manoeuvres would use the space of the arena in different ways. At the end the successful gladiators left by one exit while the dead, like the dead of other events, were dragged out through a narrow little passage called the Gate of Death.

Excavation in the arena in the nineteenth century (Plate 46) removed its surface and exposed the network of cells and corridors below (Plate 48). This was obviously the place where animals and prisoners were held. Their safe keeping before performances could be a problem. Animals that had already travelled a great distance might be weak or restive, while some human prisoners might try to escape the arena even through suicide. Symmachus, who was consul in the late fourth century CE, wrote graphically about the problem he had keeping some crocodiles alive until the games as they refused food for fifty days. When the time came for their appearance in the arena, the animals were raised in some kind of hoist, traces of which remain, and then let out through trapdoors into the ring. Other rooms below the arena must have been used by the service personnel and for the scenery and props.

It is not difficult to see how features like these in the Colosseum relate to the needs of different performers and performances, but problems remain about reconciling some ancient literary accounts of events allegedly staged with the actual archaeological remains of the building. How did such shows work, or are they perhaps only literary fictions? For instance, it is recorded that the Emperor Commodus speared 100 bears and lions in a morning from walkways especially constructed across the arena. In addition, there is reference to mock sea-battles, which would have required the arena to be flooded with water. Can the accounts of these be reconciled with the existence of the subterranean cells? One possibility is that this underground area was created only after the last recorded aquatic show in the Colosseum, and other venues were then found for them in Rome.

We have identified some of the basic requirements of the games and how they were met in the facilities of the Colosseum. TV5 and your work in Study Week 6 will look at these further.

You have also been introduced to a range of interesting sources and confronted some of the challenges they represent to modern scholars of the ancient world. Extracts C14, C15 and C16 in *Resource Book 1* have been included to provide, for those who are interested, further reading on some of the issues related to the Colosseum that we have considered in this unit. The culture of the Roman Empire is rich and varied; its surviving artistic and literary output offers a rewarding and stimulating interaction for the thoughtful student.

GLOSSARY

Grand Tour tour of classical lands popular with the British aristocracy in the eighteenth century.

Stations of the Cross sequence of devotional shrines recreating stages on Christ's route to His crucifixion.

REFERENCES

AUGUET, R. (1972) *Cruelty and Civilisation*, London, Allen & Unwin (first published as *Cruauté et civilisation: les jeux romaines*, Paris, 1970).

WIEDEMANN, T. (1992) *Emperors and Gladiators*, London, Routledge.

UNIT 6
THE COLOSSEUM TRADITION

Written for the course team by Colin Cunningham

Contents

STUDY COMPONENTS				
Weeks of study	Texts	TV	AC	Set books
1	*Illustration Book*	TV6	AC3, Bands 3 and 4	–

Aims and objectives

The aims of this unit are to:

1 initiate or add to your interest in architecture and architectural history;

2 introduce you to the basic skills of plan-reading;

3 introduce you to the classical language of architecture;

4 allow you to explore the interrelation of form and structure in two buildings;

5 demonstrate the importance of the historical context in studying a building;

6 introduce you to the concept of tradition in architectural design.

By the end of this unit you should be able to:

1 work out from a plan the relationship of different parts of a building and the nature of routes through it;

2 recognize basic elements in the classical language of architecture in the buildings studied and elsewhere;

3 understand the distinction between structural and decorative use of such forms;

4 appreciate the varying impact of convention, historical context and function on a building;

5 be aware of the sorts of factor that influence the development of architecture.

Study note: organizing your time

You should by now be beginning to work out the rhythm of study that best suits you, so I have not divided the material into separate study sessions designed to provide roughly one evening's work. The text is written continuously, with headed sections and sub-sections of different length. If you allow one evening for the cassette exercises, you will need to work through at least two sub-sections each evening to complete the unit in a week. Alternatively, you may prefer to work through one of the main sections of the unit in a single session. Whichever course you choose, I suggest you begin with a study of the cassette material on plan-reading and architectural design, since that concentrates on skills that underlie any architectural analysis. The television programme is designed to sum up the whole week's work, bringing together several of the themes considered. You will need to have the *Illustration Book* by you throughout your study of this unit.

1 INTRODUCTION

This unit offers an introduction to architectural history, and makes a link between the close focus of your study of the Colosseum (within the field of classical studies) and the wider history of culture and the built environment, which is linked to art history.

If you began your work on this block thinking that the Colosseum belongs entirely to the past, I imagine that by now you have realized what burning issues of cruelty, ecology and social organization are raised by a study of the Colosseum. You will also have seen from TV5 just how much our perception of the Colosseum is affected by its subsequent history. I hope that you have a clearer idea of how important the history of ideas and cultural history can be for us. How, though, should we react to the building itself? You might want to dismiss it on the grounds that it is largely ruinous and no longer has any real function! I believe that this would be a mistake.

Effectively you have already been studying the Colosseum through three approaches: first, as a concept; second, for its function in Roman society; and finally, as an artefact. This unit is principally concerned with exploring the place of the Colosseum building in Western architecture, that is, tracing its influence as an artefact. The Colosseum does have a modern function as a tourist attraction and place of pilgrimage, as can be seen in TV5. It is also a structure that has interested and influenced artists and architects over the centuries. It has had a significant influence on the Western architectural tradition, and one of the more important enquiries that an architectural historian needs to address is the question of the importance of tradition. After all, it is not possible to design a building without being aware of previous works that have similar functions or provide solutions to similar problems. Some buildings are recognized by later generations as key works; the Colosseum is one of the buildings that has helped to establish the conventions of what we now recognize as the **classical tradition** in Western architecture. It is the source and inspiration of many later buildings and for that reason is still relevant for us today.

It is these aspects of the Colosseum that I want to explore in this unit. I shall begin by analysing the structure of the Colosseum, and the form given to that structure. We can then move on to examine the different ways in which this form has been used by later generations. The next part of the unit will concentrate on the working of the Colosseum and more recent stadia as the functional descendants of the Roman amphitheatre. There we will also look at the influence of new structures on the form of the modern stadium. The final part of the unit, which relates closely to TV6 (*Wembley Stadium: venue of legends*), takes one stadium, Wembley, as a case study.

There are effectively two ways in which we may study a building. We can study the way a building appears or we can study the way it works and is planned and constructed. We could categorize these two approaches as the study of the **form** and the study of the **function** of a building. The two approaches are inextricably linked, but I shall be tracing the influence of these two aspects of the Colosseum separately. I believe that both aspects have influenced us and are an important element in our understanding of Western culture.

In looking at the form of the Colosseum, I shall try to show how its appearance may have a direct influence on the way we understand what is known as classical architecture, and how the patterns of classical architecture have been used at different periods. That will rely on analysis of visual evidence, which you will find in the accompanying plates in the *Illustration Book*, to which you will be referred.

However, as you know, there is a great deal more to the Colosseum than mere shapes. Although we have no exact parallel today for the entertainments that took place in the amphitheatre, the Colosseum was designed to cope with problems that do recur – the accommodation of very large numbers of people; giving a good view of the spectacle; crowd safety and control – all of which are still problems today. These are the elements that I class as the function of the Colosseum. (It is important to recognize at the outset that this is a slightly different use of the term 'function' from the one you met last week. Then you were studying the significance of the Colosseum and the spectacle of the games in relation to Roman society; now you will study the way in which the Colosseum building accommodated the uses required by Roman society.) I shall examine how these problems affect some modern stadia and we shall then consider some of the ways in which similar functional needs are met in some recently built examples. In particular, we shall look at the interaction between new materials and the sorts of structure they make possible. This, in turn, raises questions about the persistence and the relevance of the conventions established by the Colosseum.

Finally, I believe that just as we can learn a great deal about the culture and values of the Romans from an analysis of their arena, so we can find out about some of our own values and cultural priorities from a study of our nearest equivalent. Your work on this block will be completed by a study of both the form and the function of one particular stadium, the way it came to be built and how it fits into our present age. For this I have chosen Wembley, the English national stadium.

2 CASSETTE EXERCISES

Before we begin a study of the Colosseum as a building, it may be as well to make sure that you are familiar with some of the technical drawings and design features we shall need to use as evidence.

Plan-reading

CASSETTE 3, SIDES 1 AND 2, BAND 3

Listen to AC3, Sides 1 and 2, Band 3 now. This contains exercises designed to help you with studying architectural plans. You have already had to examine plans and sections of the Colosseum in Unit 5 and TV5, so there is an element of revision in this.

For convenience and ease of reference, the plates referred to and the questions asked are listed below. If any of the terms used on the cassette are unfamiliar to you, you should check the glossary at the end of this unit. ■

Plates referred to

For the cassette exercise on plan-reading, you will need to have ready the following plates. On the cassette these are referred to as Plates A–M, which correspond to Colour Plate 21 and Plates 51–59 in the *Illustration Book* as indicated. You may find it convenient to mark these plates in the *Illustration Book* with the prefix PR for plan-reading.

A	Colour Plate 21	Pantheon, Rome 118–c.128CE, section. Sir John Soane's Museum, London.
B	Plate 51	Pantheon, Rome, section. (Reproduced from *Sir Banister Fletcher's A History of Architecture*)
C	Plate 52	Pantheon, Rome, section. (Adapted from *Sir Banister Fletcher's A History of Architecture*)
D	Plate 53	Sir John Soane, plan of a mausoleum, *c.*1780. Sir John Soane's Museum, London.
E	Plate 54	Pantheon, Rome, plan. (Reproduced from *Sir Banister Fletcher's A History of Architecture*)
F	Plate 55	Colosseum, Rome, plan. (Reproduced from *Sir Banister Fletcher's A History of Architecture*)
G–J	Plate 56 (a)–(d)	Colosseum, Rome, plans at different levels. (Based on *Sir Banister Fletcher's A History of Architecture*)
K	Plate 57	Colosseum, Rome, section. (Reproduced from J.B. Ward-Perkins, *Roman Imperial Architecture*)
L	Plate 59	Colosseum, Rome.
M	Plate 58	Sir John Soane, Colosseum, Rome, diagrammatic section and part elevation, 1778–80. Sir John Soane's Museum, London.

Questions asked

You are asked to find answers to the following questions as you study the cassette.

- What are the principal differences between the two sections of the Pantheon (Plates A and B)?

- What is the basic shape of the Pantheon?

- Where is the main entrance? (Are there others?)

- What form does the main entrance take?

- What do the lines at the outer edge of the **portico** represent? (Is there any difficulty in 'reading' them?)

- What is indicated by the dotted lines in the plan?

- Where did the gladiators enter the Colosseum (Plate G)? What sort of route did they take?

- Can you detect any pattern in the way the different stairways are disposed around the building?

- How can you explain the narrowing of the stairways of the inner ring?

- How is the wall between the upper and lower tiers marked?

- What is missing from the section shown in Plate M? How can you explain the omission?

Architectural design

The next band on the cassette parallels the study material on pages 59–72 of this unit and will be useful as a reinforcement of your work. You may either study the cassette now or when you reach the section on the **articulation** of the Colosseum (p.59).

CASSETTE 3, SIDE 2, BAND 4

Listen to AC3, Side 2, Band 4 now. This contains exercises designed to help you analyse the ways in which the exteriors of buildings are articulated. The plates referred to and the questions asked are listed below. ■

Plates referred to

For the cassette exercise on architectural design you will need to have ready the following plates. On the cassette these are referred to as Plates A–R, which correspond to Colour Plates 22–25 and Plates 59–71 in the *Illustration Book* and Figure 6.2 in this text as indicated. You may find it convenient to mark these plates in the *Illustration Book* with the prefix AD for architectural design. If any of the terms used on the cassette are unfamiliar to you, you should check the glossary at the end of this unit.

A	Plate 59	Colosseum, Rome.
B	Plate 60	Tempietto San Pietro in Montorio, Rome, Bramante, 1502.
C	Plate 61	President Nicolae Ceausescu's Palace, Bucharest, 1970s and 1980s.
D	Plate 62	Seagram Building, New York, Mies van der Rohe and Philip Johnson, 1958.
E	Plate 63	Half-timbered farmhouse, Grange Farm, Abbey Dore, Herefordshire, fourteenth century and later.
F	Plate 64	Bryanston School, CDT building, Piers Gough of CZWG, 1987–8.
G	Plate 66	Canterbury Cathedral, twelfth century and later.
H	Plate 67	Parthenon, Athens, Iktinus and Kallikrates, 447–36 BCE.
I	Figure 6.2	Diagram of Greek Doric and Ionic orders.
J	Plate 65	Arch of Titus, Rome, c.81 CE.
K	Colour Plate 22	Arch of Constantine, Rome, 315 CE.
L	Plate 68	Ashmolean Museum, Oxford, C.R. Cockerell, 1841–5.
M	Colour Plate 24	King's Circus, Bath, John Wood, 1740 onwards.
N	Colour Plate 25	Elphinstone Circle (later Horniman Circle), Bombay, James Scott, 1864 onwards.
O	Colour Plate 23	Santa Maria Novella, Florence, façade by Leon Battista Alberti, 1456–70.
P	Plate 69	Palazzo del Te, Mantua, Giulio Romano, 1525 onwards.
Q	Plate 70	Louvre, Paris, east façade, Louis le Vau and Claude Perrault, 1667.
R	Plate 71	Attingham Park, Shropshire, George Steuart, 1782.

Questions asked

You are asked to find answers to the following questions as you study the cassette.

- How do the elements of architecture work to create meaning in Plate D?

- How does the site help?

- Make a note of what strikes you as unusual, interesting or even amusing in Plate F.

- How are the **columns** used in Plate H?

- What has happened to the columns in Plate J?

- Compare Plates J and K. What are their similarities? How does their use of the classical system of **orders** differ?

- What echoes of Plate K can be seen in Plate L? How has this designer varied the use of the classical language?

- Compare Plates M and N and relate them to Plate A. How have the designers managed to articulate their **façades**?

- How have the orders been used to articulate the buildings in Plates O–R? What are the different effects of the different methods of articulation?

3 THE FORM OF THE COLOSSEUM: SHAPES AND PATTERNS

You will find that a good deal of the material in this section on the structure of the Colosseum and its planning and function is familiar to you from TV5. This will mean that there is an element of revision and you may find you can work more quickly or more confidently at this point. However, you should try to resist the temptation to skip this mateial, as it was designed to reinforce an understanding of how the art of architecture 'works' and other parts of this unit will assume that you are familiar with the concepts discussed.

The structure of the Colosseum

Before we begin to consider the form, or appearance, of the Colosseum (Colour Plate 19) we need to know a little about the way it is constructed (Plate 58). The Roman engineer Vitruvius, in his book *On Architecture* written barely 100 years before the Colosseum was built, considered that architecture needed to satisfy three requirements, which he labelled 'commodity', 'firmness' and 'delight'. He meant that a building should operate easily and efficiently, providing the necessary shelter and other requirements (commodity). It must also be securely built so that it would not collapse (firmness). Finally, it should afford a pleasing appearance (delight).

Firmness depends on both the requirements of a particular function and the technology available at the time. The requirement for the Colosseum was a very large quantity of tiered seating. Previously, this had been provided either by means of temporary wooden benches or by piling up earth banks. Neither of these approaches would have worked for the Colosseum, which was to be a permanent amphitheatre for 50,000 spectators. Timber benches simply would not have sustained the weight if they had been built high enough to give all the spectators a clear view.

Equally, a bank of earth of suitable dimensions would have posed enormous problems in containing the tremendous weight of soil required. Besides, both these approaches would have made access extremely difficult.

EXERCISE

Look at the photographs, plans and sections of the Colosseum in Colour Plates 19 and 26–29 and Plates 55–59 and 72–78. What materials can you make out? How do you think this structure stands up?

DISCUSSION

The photographs show both brick and stone, which are the principal facing materials. It is not so easy to explain how the building stands up but I hope you recognized that it is not a solid bank of material. In fact, the first impression from the ground floor plan (Plate 56(a)) is that it is a honeycomb of walls and pillars; you can see from Colour Plate 29 (interior arcades) and Plate 72 (stairs and arcades; this plate also identifies the materials discussed in TV6) that the spaces are roofed with **vaults** supported on brick and stone **piers**. The brick surface of these vaults is only a facing material. The Romans were experienced in constructing semicircular vaults and domes, which they made with a version of concrete, although you will not have been able to see this material because it is usually concealed by the facing of brick or stone.

If you look at the plan shown in Plate 55, you will see that the walls and piers are all arranged in a pattern that radiates out from the centre of the arena. (All the passages between them taper slightly as they draw nearer to the arena.) The space between each radiating wall is covered with a vault. You can see the beginnings of these vaults, which have now collapsed, in the thickened tops of the walls in Colour Plate 29. At ground level there are also four passages that allow movement round the building as well as straight into it (Plate 77). These passages are covered by cross-vaults, which run in a ring right round the building. The pattern is repeated over a diminishing area on each successive floor. The structure is therefore one of load-bearing walls and piers supporting a series of vaults.

Roman concrete vaults really are extraordinarily strong. They were made by building up layers of facing material which would hold cement in place while it set. The centre of the vault was then filled with porridge-like cement, often mixed with rubble, a layer at a time. When the whole thing had set, the resulting structure was effectively one enormous piece. The brick or stone facing provided a smooth surface which could then be plastered or painted, but the real strength of the structure was in the vault. The facing could fall away and still leave the structure intact, as has happened with a number of Roman buildings. Fortunately, the structure frequently retains much of its facing, so that we can study not just its 'commodity' and 'firmness', but also the way the building elements were arranged to provide 'delight'.

You can see from the elevation in Plate 73 that the vaults are piled up in layers, and it is a tribute to the engineers of the first century CE that so much is still standing after 1900 years. It is worth bearing in mind too that all this was erected in a period of just ten years, with only wooden scaffolding and without the aid of the tall, powered cranes that are a regular part of building sites today. We may take it for granted that large, probably very large, numbers of slaves were available to do the work. Long traditions of working with the local stones and with concrete would have helped to ensure that foundations of sufficient depth were dug and that the walls and piers were thick enough to support the many thousands of tons of concrete. If you found the plans complex, just think for a moment how difficult it must have been to lay out such a large and intricate building on the ground! We can be impressed not just by the size and massiveness of this structure, but by the planning and organization that made it possible.

The next four sub-sections concentrate on what Vitruvius called 'delight' – the way the Colosseum appears. The first sub-section shows how the appearance relies on certain conventions and the next will introduce you to the way in which these conventions operate in architecture generally. We shall then see, in the following two sub-sections, how the basic shapes of the Colosseum have reappeared in a number of buildings of later eras.

The Colosseum: scale, articulation and meaning

One reason why the Colosseum has so impressed later generations, and no doubt also why it impressed the Romans, is quite simply that it is so big. The short diameter is 156.5 metres (over 500 feet), which is easy to read but much less easy to understand. That space is enclosed by a wall 48 metres (157.5 feet) high! It is worth for a moment trying to get to grips with sizes such as these. In order to give you a feeling for the **scale** of the Colosseum, it is shown in the *Illustration Book* alongside a view of the Open University (Colour Plates 19 and 20). Try to spot the figures of people shown in the foreground to the Colosseum and compare them with the figure shown in front of the Open University building. If you look at Plates 73 and 77 you will also be able to make out people beside and within the Colosseum. Look at the size of the people compared to the size of the building. This should help to make you aware of its vast scale. The massiveness of the Colosseum structure is certainly something that impressed later architects who wanted to learn from Roman building. Colour Plate 30 shows the Colosseum enclosing and dwarfing King's

Circus, Bath (Colour Plate 30), a terrace of houses built in Britain in the mid-eighteenth century.

The sense of scale is enormously important in assessing buildings. I mention it first because of the problem it set for the builders of the Colosseum in making so huge a structure fit into the cityscape of Rome. You might feel that the building itself was unattractive or daunting because of its size. On the other hand, the Romans seem to have been thoroughly proud of this building and of what went on inside it! I think the appearance of the building had something to do with this, and I want to take you through a simple exercise of **architectural analysis** to see how this might have worked. We shall concentrate on the exterior, and shall be studying how the façade was articulated.

EXERCISE

Compare the Colosseum as shown in Plates 59 and 79 (Colosseum with articulation removed). In Plate 79 the building has been altered to remove all the features that enable us to 'read' the structure, that is, to work out how it fits together, and how it has meaning. Identify the elements that can be seen in Plate 78 (elevation of a section of the Colosseum) but not in Plate 79.

DISCUSSION

Plate 79 has all the columns and **cornices**, that is, all the projecting areas, removed. If they were in reality chiselled off from the building it would make very little difference in terms of structure, but they are essential to our 'reading' of the building. Without them it appears like a vast blank wall with holes in it – perhaps rather forbidding.

This pattern was adopted by Mussolini's architects in their design for the Museum of Roman Civilization just outside Rome in 1940 (Plate 80). This is generally regarded as a fine example of fascist architecture. Many people still find it rather dull and oppressive, although it is not as big as the Colosseum.

With all its columns and cornices the Colosseum has a richness that gives interest to its great bulk, as well as expressing its imperial splendour. The impression of richness and imperial splendour is a part of the meaning of the building, and that meaning is part of the intention of the architect or builder as well as being related to function. A part of the way in which the impression given by this building is achieved is in the **articulation** of the wall surface. I think we may assume that the architects designed the exterior of this building to look attractive. However, there was a good deal more involved in this than merely adding some decoration. The architects have used a system of breaking up the façade, which makes it much easier to look at and makes it feel more approachable by humans. We need to consider exactly how this was done.

EXERCISE

Try, for instance, comparing the façade of the Colosseum with that of the Sultan Han in Turkey (Plate 81), or with the Great Mosque at Samarra in Iraq (Plate 82).

DISCUSSION

The Colosseum has vastly more openings as well as being decorated with columns all over. Both the other buildings have plainer, blanker walls, although both have decorated entrances.

There is a good reason for this, in that the Sultan Han is a defendable caravanserai, whose purpose is to provide safe shelter for travellers. All the interest is on the inside. The Great Mosque was intended to provide space set aside for worshippers, away from the distractions of the world. Again, all the interest is on the inside. In both these cases there would be less need to articulate the outside wall, since its function was to exclude.

EXERCISE

Now look at Plate 83 (El Escorial, Madrid) and consider whether this is as forbidding as the last two buildings or the plain wall of the Colosseum.

DISCUSSION

I would argue that it is slightly less so. There are rather more windows, and there is a large decorated section in the middle of the wall.

El Escorial was a monastery, but it was also a royal palace. Although it was a building designed to exclude the public at large, it was also intended to express the might and majesty of the Spanish king. Thus, some of the interest needed to be on the outside. There were certain people, such as ambassadors, who had to be allowed access, and it was necessary for them to be properly impressed by this setting for a monarch. You can see how both these aims are achieved in the way there is a great deal of blank wall, punctuated only by windows, but in the centre of the wall there is much elaboration, with columns and other decorative features around a huge doorway. Attention is drawn to this part of the wall more than to the rest as a way of marking the formal approach. This is the function of articulation. It provides a sense of order for a large façade, and enables the architect to give a building meaning.

EXERCISE

If you consider the Colosseum, do you feel the interest was on the inside or the outside? What are the implications of this for the classical tradition in architecture?

DISCUSSION

There is a sense in which the interest is on the inside. The building was intended to accommodate spectacles, which those present had to be able to see. It was also necessary to make extensive provision for public access. This is why the exterior wall is pierced with a series of arches, giving easy access to walkways around the building and to the stairs up to tiered seating. However, its simple presence in the city was a reminder of the emperor's patronage and power. So the Colosseum also has a good deal of its interest on the outside, where the wall is richly articulated. This is because it was essentially a public building. Its function – providing for the spectacle of the games – disappeared with the Romans (although we still have a need for large amphitheatres, nowadays usually called stadia), but the structure of the Colosseum still dominates the part of Rome in which it is situated. The outside was, and remained, the most visible element of it, and it is the exterior that has most influenced other generations. The ruinous nature of the interior, the loss of its function and the particular feelings caused by its association with Christian martyrdom, meant that later generations were less interested in the form and shape of the interior. However, it was difficult not to be impressed with the suggestion of imperial magnificence in the shape of the exterior façade. This was a key reason why later architects chose to use the pattern of that façade in buildings that they wanted to express grandeur.

The continual reuse of this patterns of elements, established in the classical period, helped to give buildings of later peiods meaning. It allowed them to 'speak', to convey a message of splendour and power. Thus, by association, we can speak of a 'classical language of architecture' in the forms and elements that the Romans used, and which have been copied and developed ever since.

The articulation of the Colosseum: a language of architecture

Most of the architectural terms used in this and subsequent sections are illustrated in TV5, but you may also wish to refer to a dictionary for definitions. (Any good dictionary should include all the terms mentioned here.) If you are interested in architectural history, the *Penguin*

Dictionary of Architecture (Fleming *et al.*, 1991) is probably the most accessible specialist dictionary, with many useful diagrams.

It was the exterior design, or articulation, that gave the Colosseum its meaning as a great public monument of Imperial Rome, so we need to see just how the articulation was achieved.

EXERCISE

Look at Colour Plate 28 and Plates 75 and 76 (arcades). There is a clear pattern in the divisions of the wall surface. How is the great bulk of this building divided up? Can you work out the approximate height of the divisions? Can you suggest possible reasons for it being the way it is?

DISCUSSION

I hope you were able to see that the wall is divided into four layers. This clear division of the structure into four layers makes it easy to look at, and we 'read' it as having four 'floors'. You may remember, however, that the tiers of seats inside rise in one slope with only one major break, at the top. From the section shown in Plate 74 you can see that only the major break and one of the entrances to the seating correspond to the 'floors' of the exterior. In fact, the 'floors' relate principally to the stages of the many stairways. In other words, the exterior was designed to reflect the staged progress of the access, whilst the interior was designed to reinforce the unity of the whole crowd of spectators watching the games. (However, as was described in Unit 5, the seats were, in fact, divided into five sections to reflect social distinctions.)

Each of the external divisions is roughly 40 feet high. This makes them very tall for a 'floor', but human beings would not be as completely dwarfed by a height of 40 feet as they would by one of 150 feet. Equally, a building with four 'floors' seems more approachable than one with eight or ten. So the division into four 'floors' helps the visitor to relate to the building. Each 'floor' is marked out by a pattern of arches within columns, which is called an **arcade**. The pattern of the arcade used in the Colosseum is a sophisticated design within the tradition of classical architecture, and we need to look in more detail at the 'rules' or conventions that make up that tradition.

You will probably have noticed that each arch is over the one below, with the piers rising one above the other. This reflects the structure of the interior, with its radiating series of walls and piers. It also gives a great feeling of strength (or firmness), since in all cases the voids are over other voids, and the solid parts over other solid parts.

I would say that the designers of this great building got it about right, making it imposing but not oppressive, welcoming yet large enough for the biggest crowds. What really impresses me is the regularity of the façade, with each arch framed by pillars and with an **entablature** or beam and cornice above. Another aspect of the façade that seems well thought out is the relation of the arched opening to the columns. Its width is governed by the fact that the arch itself is a semicircle. If the arches were any lower they might appear squat and crushed by the mass of the building. If they were any taller they would interrupt the line of the cornice. This is a matter of **proportion**, which is an important element in the classical tradition of architecture.

Do you notice also how each layer is distinguished from the others by the fact that the pillars are of a slightly different design? The design of these pillars was governed by sets of proportion that had become agreed over many generations of building. In fact, they derive from Greek architecture developed more than five centuries before the Colosseum was built. The designs are known as the orders and they have been important in Western architecture since they were first developed. It would be useful to become familiar with the orders, so that you can discover how they have influenced Western architecture.

The Greeks recognized three orders – Doric, Ionic and Corinthian – and the Romans considered that there should be two further orders – Tuscan (rather like Greek Doric but unfluted and with a base) and Composite (like Corinthian but with a **capital** combining the richness of both Ionic and Corinthian). The columns of the Roman orders are illustrated in Figure 6.1. The easiest way to distinguish them is by the pattern of their capitals and whether or not the shafts of the columns are fluted. However, there is more to consider than this, as each order consists of both a column and an entablature and they differ in their proportions (ratio of width to height). Each column consists of a base (except Greek Doric), a shaft and a capital and each entablature is divided into two elements, an **architrave** and a **frieze** (see the diagram of Greek Doric and Ionic orders shown in Figure 6.2).

EXERCISE

In order to confirm that you can identify the different orders, find Plates 60, 65, 67, 68, 70, 71 and 84–87 (Tempietto San Pietro in Montorio; Arch of Titus, Rome; Parthenon, Athens; Ashmolean Museum, Oxford; Louvre, Paris; Attingham Park, Shropshire; British Museum, London; Cumberland Terrace, London; Leeds Town Hall; Euston Arch, London) and check them against the diagrams in Figures 6.1 and 6.2.

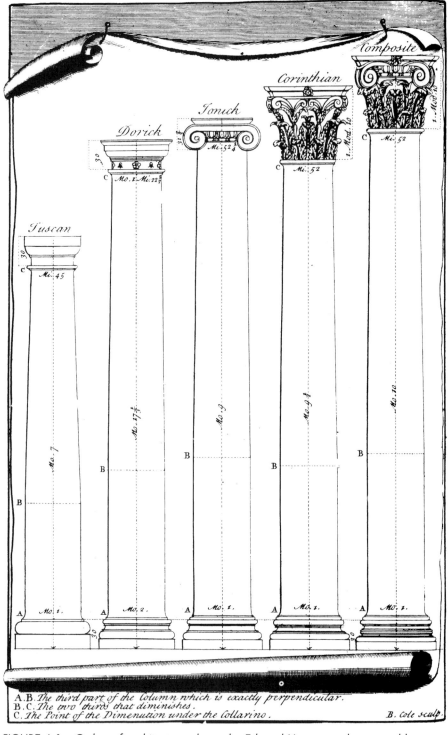

FIGURE 6.1 *Orders of architecture, drawn by Edward Hoppus and engraved by B. Cole, from Andrea Palladio, I Quattro Libri dell'Architettura (The Four Books of Architecture), edited by Edward Hoppus, London, 1773, pl. VIII. (Reproduced by permission of the Syndics of the Cambridge University Library)*

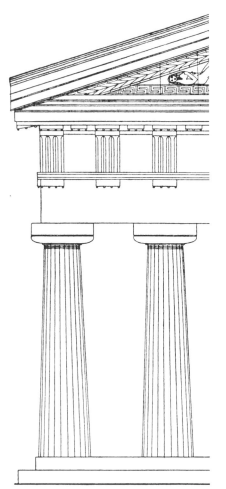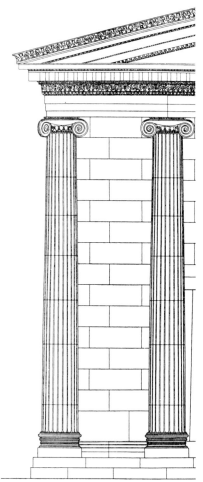

FIGURE 6.2   *Diagram of Greek Doric and Ionic orders:*
restored elevation of Temple of Artemis, Corfu, after G. Rodenwalt, Korkyra, Archaische
Bauten und Bildwerke, *Berlin, 1939–40, vol.1, pl.26,*
restored elevation of front of shrine, Temple of Apollo, Didyma, after T. Wiegand,
Didyma, *Berlin, 1941, vol.1, pl.33,*
adaptations by Donald Bell-Scott. (© Penguin Books, reproduced from A. W. Lawrence,
Greek Architecture, *2nd edn, Harmondsworth, Penguin Books, 1967, figs 61 and 111)*

DISCUSSION

Below is the identification of the orders shown.

60	Tempietto San Pietro in Montorio	Roman Doric or Tuscan
65	Arch of Titus	Composite
67	Parthenon	Greek Doric
68	Ashmolean Museum	Ionic
70	Louvre east façade	Corinthian
71	Attingham Park	Ionic
84	British Museum	Ionic

85	Cumberland Terrace	Ionic
86	Leeds Town Hall	Corinthian
87	Euston Arch	Greek Doric

I hope you also noticed that there are wide variations in the proportions as well as the spacing of the columns. The columns of Euston Arch are squat and solid compared with those of Attingham Park, for instance. One of the most important characteristics of the classical orders is this proportion, which governs the internal relationship of the various parts that make up the order *and* the relative heights and widths of the different orders. The internal relationships are based on the fact that the dimensions of each part of the order (and often of the whole building) are multiples or fractions of the base diameter of the column. In the Doric order the column is generally only 4–7 diameters tall, whereas the Ionic column, with its entablature, is generally 9–10 diameters tall. The Corinthian order is usually more slender still.

Doric and Tuscan orders, therefore, give an appearance of sturdiness to a building, while Ionic and Corinthian orders tend to make buildings appear rich and elegant. The spacing of the columns is important too, since closely set columns will give an appearance of strength but will tend to obscure views out of a building. On the other hand, open, widely spaced columns may give a sense of lightness but can also appear insubstantial. You can see some of these differences in the plates cited above.

The effect of 'rules' such as these for the use of classical orders in designing buildings has been considerable. Sometimes architects will deliberately break the 'rules' for effect (see Plate 69) or out of ignorance. However, the general result is that viewers are aware of proportional relationships (even if we never work them out exactly!) and buildings appear logically put together. Of course, such a systematic method of design brings its problems and can be restrictive. For designers to be sure that their ordering of façades will work, that all the parts will fit together, they need to know in advance the sizes and proportions of the various parts. Otherwise there will be a risk that in a building like the Colosseum the exterior will work out at seventy-nine and a bit arches rather than the precise eighty that the Colosseum has! Precise measuring of the exterior circuit would allow the designer to calculate a figure for the span of each arch and its piers. The dimensions of the piers would control the width of the columns, and, according to the 'rules' of the orders, this in turn would control the height of the order, or the 'floor'.

AGSG, ch.2, sect.3.5, 'What if you get stuck?'

The columns are not themselves the structural elements of the building, although they give the appearance of being structural. It is difficult to see columns without thinking of them as posts, and it is difficult to see an entablature without thinking of it as a beam. However, you have probably already noticed that the columns of the Colosseum are not real columns at all, but merely **half-columns** built as part of the wall surface. Their function, as we considered earlier, is to articulate the surface of the building. Their disposition derives from the traditional proportions of the orders.

The apparent logic of the Colosseum is not, then, simply a matter of dividing up the height. The choice of the orders itself provided a framework for the divisions of the whole building. This classical language of architecture is capable of considerable subtlety. For instance, do you recall that there are different orders at different levels of the building? Check back and you will see that the lowest tier is formed with a Tuscan, sometimes referred to as Doric, order (that is the sturdiest), above that is an Ionic order (noticeably more slender), and above that the most slender of all, Corinthian (which is repeated for the upper plain wall). This pattern of combining the orders also became standard.

AGSG, ch.2, sect.4, 'Remembering'

You do not need to remember all the details of these designs. However, it is important that you understand how this method of designing gave the architect control over the proportions and relationships of all the parts of the building. We shall now consider some of the ways in which the language of architecture has been used over the centuries.

Reusing the language: Roman examples

We have already seen that the orders that underlie the classical language of architecture derive originally from Greek temple buildings. In fact, you may have noticed that the **temple frontispiece** (a low gable or **pediment** supported on a row of columns) features in several of the examples I gave you to identify the orders. It is there in the Parthenon (Plate 67), which is a Greek temple, but it reappears in the Louvre, Attingham Park, the British Museum and Euston Arch (Plates 70, 71, 84 and 87), and there is one in the background on Cumberland Terrace (Plate 85). The temple frontispiece is one of the more important motifs in the development of Western classical architecture. The combination of arch and **colonnade** that decorates the Colosseum is another, and we shall be tracing that motif in this and the following section and considering the effects achieved and the intentions of the designers who reused or developed the system.

In Greek architecture the columns were used as a part of the structure, like stone posts supporting stone beams. Roman architects often abandoned this use of columns, because they were able to support their buildings with concrete vaults. For them the chief value of the orders was as a means of articulating surfaces and decorating buildings. They therefore used both columns and **attached** or half-columns (like the ones on the Colosseum) and **pilasters**. This use of the orders gave them a richly varied means of designing the façades of buildings.

EXERCISE

Look at Colour Plates 22 (Arch of Constantine, Rome) and 31 (Trajan's Forum, Rome), Plates 88 (Porta Nigra, Trier) and 89 (Amphitheatre, Arles) and Figure 6.3. How do these buildings use the decorative system of arch and column? How do they differ from the Colosseum?

FIGURE 6.3 *Set designed by M. Ceroli for production of* Verdi's Il Trovatore *in Verona arena (amphitheatre). (Photograph: Index/Pizzi)*

DISCUSSION

If you checked the captions, you will have noticed that these buildings are all of the Roman period, so it would be reasonable to expect that they would use the contemporary system of articulation in similar ways. (You may also remember that in TV5 the articulation of the Colosseum was compared to that of the Theatre of Marcellus (Rome, 23–13 BCE), which may well have inspired the builders of the Colosseum.)

The Arch of Constantine was designed merely as a focus for processions. Not surprisingly, it uses columns to frame the arch that is the main element of the structure. Notice how the columns are made even more clearly into decorative elements. They stand clear of the structure, and the entablature has to be brought forward to sit on top of them. Their only function is to support statues. Such attention to decoration clearly fits with the design intention.

Trajan's Forum has the curve of the building reversed, and a more complicated rhythm of openings. Those on the upper floor occur both over the lower ones and over the gaps between them. The pattern of columns could not therefore rise the whole height of the building, although there are still pilasters used like columns to frame each opening. The openings on the upper floor even have miniature pediments over some of the arches.

The Porta Nigra at Trier uses a similar system of columns and arches to frame openings, but only the two gateways are on the same scale as the arches of the Colosseum. The amount of space between the columns and the small openings of the upper storeys may seem slightly less elegant, and there are no openings between the columns on the wings of the ground floor. On the other hand, like all the examples, this gateway does use the discipline of the proportions of the orders.

Although neither is as vast, the two amphitheatres are most like the Colosseum. This is not surprising, since they perform exactly the same function as the Colosseum but are later examples of this type of building. However, the present-day uses of the amphitheatres need have no relation to the pattern of the structure. It affects only the interiors.

One important point is that, where these buildings have different functions from that of the Colosseum, their designers have needed to adapt the basic rhythm of column and arch to different purposes. The fact that this was quite possible reflects the widespread applicability of this classical language of architecture, which was used in many other ways and other places by later generations. The consensus as to acceptable proportions gave the architecture of the Roman era great consistency and, many would argue, great quality. Certainly, the use of this system is a characteristic of Roman architecture and so it will have seemed important to any who were interested in Roman architecture or who felt that Roman architecture was to be valued. As we shall see, the latter has been a fairly common opinion in the last six centuries.

Reusing the language: Western architecture in later centuries

The last few examples showed you some of the ways in which the Romans made use of one key system of articulation in their architecture. So large and important was the Colosseum, where this system was most effectively worked out, that it had an immense influence on designers of later centuries. In the centuries following the break-up of the Roman Empire (roughly from the fifth to the twelfth centuries CE) many of the skills of the Romans were lost or abandoned. Although many fine structures were built, their designers seem to have been uninterested in, or unaware of, the precision of the traditional systems of proportion. Colour Plate 32 shows a thirteenth-century palace from Constantinople (now Istanbul), still at that date ruled by a 'Roman' emperor (it was not until 1453 that the city was finally absorbed into the Turkish Empire). Here, although there are arches and columns, the relation of the arches to each other does not seem to be the result of a strict geometrical logic. The central pier of the wall is decorated with a pilaster, but the pairs of arches are directly supported by a column in the middle. It is as though parts of the original Roman system were being used, but the system as a whole could be ignored. Although there is rich decoration, there is little overall unity. You can see how the original idea becomes obscured or debased in Plate 90 (Church of the Intercession on the Nerl, Bogolyubovo), where the vestiges of columns and arches have become simply a surface decoration with no sense of classical proportion and the different layers of the building run into one.

EXERCISE

Now look at Figure 6.4. Do you see any similarities between this and the Colosseum? What differences can you make out?

FIGURE 6.4 *Peterborough Cathedral, elevation of interior bays of choir, 1118–44. (Reproduced from Sir Banister Fletcher's A History of Architecture, © British Architectural Library, The Royal Institute of British Architects)*

DISCUSSION

At first glance there seem to be a number of similarities, and I suspect that the masons who built this building believed they were working in the best tradition of architecture. However, it is most unlikely that they ever saw the Colosseum, and, although I have chosen an illustration that stresses the similarities, there are significant departures from the classical tradition. Figure 6.4 shows two bays of a building of three storeys, each of which has round-headed arches, and which are divided by tall, thin columns and horizontal bands. Thus far it is very like the Colosseum, but if you remember that the proportions of the columns were an important element in the Roman system, the differences begin to appear. The central column is very much thinner than would have been acceptable to a Roman architect. Indeed, we would call it a **shaft** or a **rib** not a column. The horizontal divisions are not as deep as on the Colosseum and they would be classed as **string courses** rather than entablatures. In addition, the paired arches are directly supported by columns and the arches of the top tier are of different sizes.

What you are looking at is an early medieval structure, in a style known as Romanesque, which indicates its derivation from classical Rome. I do not want to suggest that Romanesque is in any way inferior to Roman, but it is important to recognize that it is different. The logic of its proportions comes from the ribbed structure that eventually developed into the Gothic system. In fact, Peterborough Cathedral stands at the start of the Gothic tradition, whose language was based on vaulting and **buttresses** rather than columns and cornices. It was not until the Renaissance that the classical tradition was fully recovered.

EXERCISE

Look at Colour Plates 23, 33 and 34 (Santa Maria Novella, Florence; Pazzi Chapel, Santa Croce, Florence; Ospedale degli Innocenti, Florence) and Plates 91–93 (St Peter's Square, Rome; Palazzo Rucellai, Florence; Basilica, Vicenza). Do you see any similarities to the Colosseum in these buildings? Can you suggest any reason why they might have been influenced by the Colosseum?

DISCUSSION

The similarities are not that close but I hope you can make out that each of these structures uses some of the elements of the Colosseum system. There are clearly columns or pilasters, which are not too far different in proportion from Roman ones, and their capitals are close copies of Roman capitals – Corinthian in the case of Santa Maria Novella and the Pazzi Chapel. In these buildings, the arches are not as neatly related to the height of the columns as in the Colosseum but the echo is there. The colonnade of St Peter's Square has hardly any echoes of the Colosseum, since it is only of one storey and there are no arches associated with the columns. On the other hand, the basic form of the colonnade may be seen as reminiscent of the Colosseum, albeit inside out. In fact, I would argue that if this encircling colonnade suggests the arms of the church enfolding the faithful, there may well be a deliberate echo of the Colosseum, where a pagan empire enclosed and slaughtered Christians in the amphitheatre. If you find this argument convincing, it is an example of the power of association in architecture.

There is certainly a deliberate attempt to capture associations in the Palazzo Rucellai and the Basilica. The Palazzo Rucellai has three 'floors' divided up with a surface pattern very like the Colosseum. It is probable that this was a conscious attempt to make reference to the buildings and civilization of the once great Roman Empire. The columns and entablatures of the Basilica at Vicenza seem to me even closer derivatives. Did you notice also that both these buildings adopt the same principle of stacking up the columns in diminishing order of the stoutness of their proportions – Doric or Tuscan on the base, Ionic above and Corinthian where there is a third storey?

If you agree that the last two buildings in particular seem to be a deliberate copy of Roman architecture, the reason may have something to do with the fact that all these buildings are in Italy. During the period we call the Renaissance, Roman remains were increasingly studied and copied. In fact, the Basilica at Vicenza was designed by the architect who drew the original diagram of the classical orders on which Figure 6.2 is based. It was during the Renaissance that the classical language of architecture became a sort of international style, with versions in all the countries of Europe. By the eighteenth century this language was being used in all countries that had been touched by Western civilization. Thus, there are classical buildings in America and in India. The language continued to be used in the nineteenth century and the spread of empires such as the British meant that classical buildings could be found in almost all parts of the world (see Colour Plates 25 and 35 (Elphinstone Circle, Bombay; General Staff Headquarters, St Petersburg) and Plates 94–97 (Cabildo, New Orleans; The White House, Washington, D.C.; Chevron Barracks, Colombo; Park Crescent, London)).

Of course, not all of these examples were based solely on the Colosseum and there needed to be adaptations to suit different circumstances. Different climates, different materials and different functions have all had an effect. The Spanish Cabildo (town hall) in New Orleans, for instance, combines the temple frontispiece with an arcade and columns on two storeys. As the classical 'rules' suggest, the columns are Tuscan below and Ionic above, but they are all in the form of flat pilasters, and the upper arches are slightly flattened to allow the greatest amount of window (and thus intake of light and air) in the rooms. The White House is probably more familiar, but have you ever noticed how its columns ignore the storeys and rise the full height of the building? They provide a deep verandah at both ground floor and first floor level, which is a considerable asset in hot summer weather. The barracks in Sri Lanka are almost contemporary with the White House, yet they are very different. The pattern of pilasters and blind arcading does, I think, echo the Colosseum, but there are only a few small openings. This is partly for security, but also to keep the heat out. The other buildings, however, seem to be further from any direct influence of Roman architecture, although I hope you will agree that the use of attached columns and arched windows in Elphinstone Circle in Bombay and the curved shapes and arches of the General Staff Building in St Petersburg and Park Crescent in London bear some slight similarity to the rhythms of the Colosseum or of Roman triumphal arches. Yet all these last three effectively turn the Colosseum inside out.

The echo of the form of the Colosseum is even clearer in the mid eighteenth-century King's Circus in Bath (Colour Plate 24). Its designer was making a deliberate attempt to create a piece of townscape on a Roman model (although he confused the amphitheatre with the chariot race track in calling this a 'circus'). The importance of this attitude among British architects in the late eighteenth and early nineteenth centuries is evidenced by Colour Plate 30 (the Colosseum enclosing King's Circus, Bath) and it was a design recipe that had its followers, as you can see from Colour Plate 25 and Plate 97, where the curved shape and use of columns still hark back ultimately to the Colosseum.

However, by the end of the eighteenth century there were so many possible sources – Roman, Italian Renaissance, British, French and Spanish seventeenth- and eighteenth-century buildings, books and so on – that an architect could assemble a design in a bewildering variety of ways whilst still remaining more or less in the classical tradition. It was rather like a huge river eventually spreading out into an enormous delta. Many critics of classical architecture would argue that the delta was pretty shallow and silted up! However, that is because the original functions of the Roman buildings had been forgotten – they were certainly no longer needed – and so the precise systems of Roman design were rapidly becoming inappropriate. There is, or should be, a connection between style and function in architecture. When that is lost, the style may become a sterile surface decoration devoid of meaning. Plate 98 (bull ring, Malaga) shows you an example of what, I think, is the only type of building to continue the original function of the Colosseum. Oddly enough it makes less use of the Colosseum language than all my other examples. Perhaps that is an indication of Spanish concentration on the activity inside rather than on imperial-style display.

The purpose of a reused language

Before we turn to the function of buildings, it is worth pausing and considering why so many generations in so many countries might want to copy a set of conventions, or style of building, developed in Greece and adapted by the Romans. I think one reason is that the Roman Empire included most of Western Europe and so there was some direct contact with the original tradition. However, the principal impetus was given in the Renaissance, when the philosophical texts of the Greeks and Romans were rediscovered. The values and achievements of the ancient world came to be considered as the best models for current activity. This attitude had its effect in architecture as in other fields.

In particular, in architecture, the classical systems were used for prestigious buildings such as churches and palaces. Once established as the language of grand architecture, the classical language had obvious attractions for anyone wishing to associate themselves with the princely classes, and by implication with the achievements of the Roman Empire. The system of designing with columns that was originally developed by the Greeks for the temples of their gods was adapted by the Romans for their temples, palaces and other great buildings. This legacy justified the assumption of subsequent architects that to design using the classical language of architecture was to design a building that would display prestige. Although we might no longer believe that this system is the only way to demonstrate quality or prestige, it should be admitted that prestige may be an important factor in the design of a building.

4 PLANNING AND FUNCTION

We should remember that architecture has to do with the ways in which the forms of buildings together with their functions achieve meaning for their societies. We have considered the power of convention in determining the forms of buildings, and seen how the proliferation of different sources gradually allowed architects freedom to build variations on an original theme. We now need to turn to the function of the Colosseum, and to see where the design problems that had to be overcome have occurred in other structures.

The Colosseum: access and egress

It can certainly be argued that the Colosseum, an imperial project, was intended partly to display the power and prestige of the emperor. However, there is much more to the building than mere prestige. It also had to work as an arena. Design to fulfil this purpose is the functional aspect of architecture I mentioned earlier.

The first, and most important, element to be considered would, I suppose, have been visibility, and I am sure you will agree that this was adequately achieved, since there were no pillars between any spectator and the spectacle. You have also seen how the divisions of the seating reflected Roman society, giving the best seats to males of the highest ranks. Another important functional element would be shelter, although in the case of the Colosseum shelter from sun was needed more than shelter from rain. We know that there was some sort of shelter, called a *velarium*, and you can make out in Plate 75 the fixings for the masts that supported this (see also TV5).

EXERCISE

Do you feel that the requirement to fulfil these two functions (visibility and shelter) adequately explains the shape and structure of the Colosseum?

DISCUSSION

You may well think that these functions account for the oval shape, the clear sweep of the seats and the enclosing walls of the building. However, if you look at the plan shown in Plate 55 or check back to the plan-reading exercise on AC3, you might wonder why so much effort was put into the complicated arrangement of radiating passages and stairways. The seating arrangements were constructed partly to accommodate the different ranks of Roman society, but also as an efficient mechanism for getting people safely in and out. If you have ever attended a football match or some other mass gathering in a modern stadium you will be aware that there are huge difficulties in achieving this.

EXERCISE

Check back to the sub-section on the structure of the Colosseum to remind yourself of the size of crowd the Colosseum could accommodate. Was that likely to cause problems?

DISCUSSION

Although the Colosseum was designed to accommodate a very large crowd, there are larger stadia today. We do know that there were problems with crowds in Roman amphitheatres. You have already considered the riot at Pompeii (in TV5), and the collapse of some wooden amphitheatre seating at Fidenae was a major disaster recorded by the Roman writer, Tacitus. With these horror stories in people's minds, it is not surprising that the emperor required his architects to devise an easy and effective means of entry and exit. This element of the function certainly explains the extraordinarily complex plan and honeycomb structure.

Crowds and architecture: function, structure and design

It is easy to see that different climates, different materials and different functions may require changes in a basic architectural vocabulary. However, similar functional constraints will require similar solutions whatever the architectural language. A structure I would consider as basically similar in function to the Colosseum is the football ground or the sports stadium. Stadia are very much a part of our present-day culture and we might ask whether we can learn anything from parallels with their Roman prototype. I think we need to consider three questions.

1   How close are the parallels of function?

2   Do similar functional problems lead to similar structures?

3   Have advances in technology led to any change in form?

Parallels of function

It is interesting to note that many Scottish football grounds have oval seating (see Plate 106), whereas most English grounds (although not Wembley) have a rectangular pattern of stands, although both enclose rectangular grounds. The oval form is closer to the structure of the Colosseum, and has the added advantage that there is room for more people on the curved section at each end, even if some are slightly further from the goal line. In addition, the oval shape has meant that many Scottish grounds, like the oval arena at Wembley, have been able to accommodate a variety of different facilities, such as running tracks or cycle tracks, and Wembley has been used for the Olympic Games. You might argue that this makes them slightly more like the Colosseum but I think that there is a subtler point. Grounds that can only accommodate football will be of interest only to the sector of society that wants to watch football. These grounds will thus be designed with this sector of society (and its economic power) in mind, and may be of less interest to society as a whole. Although the football-going public is (or certainly was) a large sector of British society, the specialist function of football grounds sets them apart from the Colosseum, whose spectacles evidently interested most sectors of Roman Society and accommodated a variety of types of entertainment.

Either type of ground can tell us a good deal about the sector(s) of society for which it was designed. With the growth in popularity of multiple-use stadia, with all-seater grounds, I think it is interesting to consider both how far these have needed to adopt the same functional conventions as the Colosseum, and whether the formal conventions have anything to offer football grounds today. An answer to this last question may throw interesting light on the importance of architecture in our society.

EXERCISE

Consider Plates 99 and 100 (Newcastle United Football Ground, St James's Park, west stand, exterior and interior). What sorts of material are used? Can you think of any other buildings that are at all similar in appearance? What are the implications of this?

DISCUSSION

The exterior is clad with corrugated iron, an industrial material. (It was built in 1906 at a cost of just over £8000. Newcastle United's next new stand was not built until 1972, when it cost £430,000!) The nearest equivalent in appearance, at least to the exterior, would be some sort of industrial structure – the building is not unlike some of the older steel mills. The interior is easily recognizable as a spectator stand, but do you notice how it is given some dignity by the curved pediment shape that forms the front of the commentary box? This is, however, far removed from the temple pediments we have seen elsewhere. You can also see that the front of the stand is laid out for standing spectators only. This was common until fairly recently and it implies a different attitude to the comfort that spectators might deserve.

I would suggest that the implication is that this structure was designed on a limited budget for those who had not much money to spend on tickets. It does not set out to be grand architecture, and would not make an impact on the city like the Colosseum. You could categorize the distinction as being that between 'polite' or show architecture and the everyday shapes of industrial building.

The most recent Newcastle United stand (Plate 101) is much more elaborate, and strikingly modern, but that is the result of changes that have taken place largely within living memory. I want to take a closer look at this development. In fact, the last sixty or so years have seen a huge improvement in the facilities provided by football grounds and a corresponding increase in the elaboration and impressiveness of their stadia. Huddersfield Town Football Club, for instance, has one of the finest sets of modern stands in the country (see Plate 102). Yet, when the club was established in 1908, the dressing-rooms were in an old tramcar and the only stand was an unroofed wooden affair. The first grandstand, rather like that at Newcastle, was designed in 1910. It lasted until 1950, when it burned to the ground in fifteen minutes.

Similar problems, similar structures?

You might assume that one large crowd is much like another, whether a Roman one or a modern one. Whilst I would agree to some extent, I think that there are complicating factors in the way that crowds are viewed as a part of society. In the Colosseum, the emperor and the consuls (or their representatives) were always present, and all ranks of society attended the shows, with the élite carefully allotted the best seats. Today, although the prices of all-seater stadia are more expensive than the old terraces (it cost £60,000 a year to rent a corporate box at Wembley at 1996 prices), there is less differentiation of status in seating in football stadia, except for the directors' boxes. I would regard it as an encouraging sign of democracy that all ranks of society can go together to such a venue, but that begs the question of whether all ranks do go. There is a risk that those who do not attend football matches might view the fans who do as a class apart. There is evidence of this attitude, I think, in the amount of attention given to segregating the different supporters, and in the assumption in some parts of the press that football hooliganism is the sort of thing we must expect. At one extreme there is almost a feeling that football supporters are a lower breed of individual!

If, as this view would suggest, football fans are to be considered as rabble, it must be admitted that the stadium acts as a sort of corral in which they can be safely allowed to let off steam while the match is on. This focuses attention on the link between crowd safety and crowd control, and it is as well to think of some recent examples of other uses to which stadia have been put in controlling various groups of people. The Pinochet regime of Chile found a football stadium an ideal location for holding large numbers of prisoners temporarily. If spectators can view the whole pitch, so can guards. As I write this there are reports that this has also occurred in Bosnia. Equally, if we move a little back in history, it was in vast stadia such as the Olympiastadion and the adjacent Maifeld in Berlin that Hitler found he could most effectively manipulate the crowds that swept his National Socialist Party on towards the achievement of their new order (Plates 103 and 105, Olympiastadion, Berlin).

If you are surprised at the direction this discussion is taking, it is worth remembering that we have distinguished two aspects of the meaning of function: first, the way in which a building houses the activities it is designed for, and second, the broader aspect, discussed as a part of last week's study – the place of the building and the institutions it housed as part of society. We need, therefore, in assessing the place of stadia in our society, to consider all the uses they have been put to by modern societies. We may find there are parallels with some of the less palatable aspects of Roman society. We may also, by examining the attitudes underlying the building of such stadia, reach a better understanding of the scope and importance of architecture in any society.

Of course, crowds can be frightening and unpredictable. Have you ever been caught in a crowded rush-hour train? In the Tokyo rush-hour the trains are so full that the transport company employs burly men to push commuters into them before the doors are shut. I have already mentioned examples of the dangers of crowds and attendant disasters in the Roman world. We have had the same experiences in more recent times. For instance, when a football crowd in the Nepalese national stadium tried to seek shelter during a thunderstorm, 100 people were trampled to death and 700 were injured. In the United Kingdom, Ibrox Park Stadium, in Glasgow, has had some six disasters, the first being in 1902 when 26 people were killed and 550 injured following the collapse of a newly erected wooden stand. (This is uncannily like the collapse of the Roman amphitheatre at Fidenae.) The failure to separate rival fans in Heysel Stadium (Plate 104) in 1985 led to tragic rioting. Perhaps the most graphic stadium tragedy that most of us will remember was the Hillsborough disaster of 1989, when 95 people died from crushing and asphyxiation in a surge against the barriers.

These last three examples show how stadia have failed to accommodate climate, failed in structure and failed to provide proper access for the huge crowds. The direct result of the last tragedy, following the report of Lord Justice Taylor, was a set of regulations designed to ensure adequate seating and crowd space in all major football stadia. Indeed, there have usually been some developments as the result of each major incident. In fact, over the last ten years or so, the major football clubs of the United Kingdom have become involved in a campaign of rebuilding that, considering them all together, is substantially greater than the original building work undertaken for the Colosseum. The major advances have been in shelter (protection from the climate) and seating and access (safe movement of people). There have been no recent structural failures in UK stadia.

In this context, the Colosseum is impressive, for we know of no major disasters there. Disasters in modern stadia seem to have led to radical redesigning, which was not necessary for the Colosseum because the design features needed were already there. There is also now the move towards all-seater stadia, and the Colosseum was an all-seater stadium. There has been the adoption of fireproof building materials, which the Colosseum had. There has been greater attention to ease of entry and exit, which had been central to the very plan and structure of the Colosseum from the start.

We are left with our third question: have advances in technology led to any change in form? That is the issue we shall deal with in the next section.

The football stadium: architecture, structure and meaning

The old-style football stands, now remembered with nostalgia by some, had no seats and only occasional crush barriers (Plate 106, Terraces at Hampden Park). Where there were stands they were often basic structures and there were few other facilities beyond the changing-rooms for the teams, perhaps a shop and a bar. The concentration was entirely on the football, and there was little place for luxury.

EXERCISE

Look at Plates 104 and 106–110 (Heysel Stadium, Brussels; Terraces at Hampden Park; Portsmouth Football Ground, Fratton Park; Valley Parade Ground, Bradford; Derby City Football Ground; Blackpool, timber stand), noting their respective dates. What facilities can you distinguish? What do you consider the chief changes over time? Do you see any parallels with the original Colosseum?

DISCUSSION

Clearly, there is no right answer to these questions and in each case there will be much that you cannot see from one photograph. The entrance to Heysel Stadium, built to commemorate Belgium's one hundredth anniversary of independence, makes a great gesture of formality and public display. You cannot see what facilities are behind the pillared façade, but it is safe to assume that they are better than those in Newcastle United's old west stand (Plates 99 and 100). The early stands (Plate 110) seem to be little more than sheds, and the open terraces (Plate 106) offer little more than the ability to see the pitch. The entrance to Portsmouth's Football Ground is decorated in mock Tudor style but does not relate to the massive shed of the stand behind. The stand at Bradford seems to bear almost no relation to the Colosseum, but it is a single stand rather than a complete stadium. Many grounds have been built in this way, one stand at a time, with complete redevelopment taking many years. There is an obvious economic advantage in this approach. Few football clubs had the sort of financial backing that was available to the builders of the Colosseum, and it is no accident that the design for a complete stadium at Derby was never built. The design is the only one we know has extra facilities (and that only from the caption). Perhaps the closest parallel to the Colosseum is to be found at Heysel Stadium, where the exterior was designed to make a public political statement as well as to provide good facilities for football.

The recent spate of rebuilding has resulted in larger and grander stands, with more seating, so that our football grounds have also become imposing structures. In fact, UK football has undergone the same sort of transformation in its buildings as the Roman amphitheatres underwent in the first centuries CE. The requirements of crowd safety have led to a gradual rebuilding and improvement of football grounds. In this section we shall consider what the architectural effects of this are, what conventions have helped in the transformation, and what freedoms the designers of the new stadia have been able to use. It is worth remembering that, especially in the UK, rebuilding has mostly been done one stand at a time. There have, however, been a number of new stadia designed as complete entities. It might be expected that these would give more scope for architectural display and you might therefore anticipate that complete stadia would share more of the architectural conventions of the Colosseum.

EXERCISE

Look at the stands and stadia illustrated in Colour Plate 36 (Chelsea Football Ground, London) and Plates 101, 102, 111 and 112 (Newcastle United Football Ground, St James's Park, new north stand; Alfred MacAlpine Stadium, Huddersfield; Parc des Princes, Paris; Stadio Communale, Florence). How do these differ from the earlier stands exemplified by those at Newcastle (Plate 99) and Blackpool (Plate 110)? Do they owe anything to the formal conventions of the Colosseum (the classical language of architecture)? Can you suggest reasons why they might differ?

DISCUSSION

All the stands and stadia seem to me much more modern than the old west stand at Newcastle and the one at Blackpool. They also look much grander, more in the nature of 'show' architecture. It is difficult to see anything in the views I have chosen that relates to the Colosseum, although the functions are similar. There is certainly not much in the way of the classical language of architecture. The reason is that all these structures make use of new systems of construction. They are of steel or reinforced concrete (concrete over a steel frame), with **cantilevered** roofs.

These stadia were all designed to accommodate greater crowds, in greater comfort and with a better view of the pitch than the old football stands. The Chelsea stand rises to three tiers, with a steep rake, and the topmost seats dizzily high. The stands at Huddersfield are supported beneath a curved arch that runs the length of the pitch, with striking towers at the corners for spotlights. Both of these make use of steel, a modern material that allows a lightweight frame with very widely spaced supports. Thus, there was no need for the series of posts that supported the roof at Newcastle. (You can see similar posts in the view of Wembley Stadium shown in Plate 113.)

At Parc des Princes, this form of construction is applied to the whole stadium, giving a completely integrated appearance like some vast sea urchin. You might feel that the Parc des Princes stadium does have some echoes of the Colosseum, but I think that these do not go much beyond the elliptical shape. In fact, the sea-urchin-like ribs are similar to the supports of the stand at Florence, and they make use of the same structural material, reinforced concrete. The stand at Florence makes dramatic use of the cantilever principle to which reinforced concrete is so well suited. This shape would have been impossible to build in stone or Roman cement.

To sum up, it seems that these modern stadia owe very little to the Colosseum: they no longer speak the classical language of architecture. On the other hand, they are all large enough to have a major impact on the areas in which they are built and, in that sense, they make similar architectural gestures to the Colosseum, expressing the status and economic power of the clubs concerned.

These stadia draw their appearance from the nature of their constructional system. Steel and reinforced concrete are used in a different way from stone and brick, and so a different aesthetic is developed. The huge reinforced concrete frames make their own pattern, as do the lightweight straight lines of the steel. The appearance is very different from the arches and columns (originally posts) of the Colosseum. The other element of this modern aesthetic derives from the functions of the stadia. The most striking parts, in my view, are the spreading roofs (perhaps like the lost *velarium* of the Colosseum) that indicate we now expect to be able to watch football in shelter. Other elements also help to determine the way these stadia look. The San Siro stadium in Milan (Plate 115) is dominated by its great steel roof structure and cylindrical stair towers. Another prominent feature is formed by the sloping access ramps along each side. The roof and stair towers belong to the latest extension to the building, on top of an older stadium. In that sense San Siro nicely parallels the Colosseum, which as you saw in Unit 5 was also extended upwards. The access ramps belong to an early stage of new building, an extension of the original stadium, which took its capacity from 65,000 to 100,000 people. The access ramps offer yet another parallel with the Colosseum, in that the patterns of both exteriors are determined by the routes of access. In other words, the language of their architecture expresses parallel functions, although not with similar forms.

The use of steel frames and reinforced concrete and the advent of cantilevered or suspended structures has meant that our stadia can be much lighter structures than the Colosseum. Nonetheless, the problems of seating large crowds with uninterrupted views and of providing access for huge numbers have tended to mean that similar solutions are needed to those found by the Romans. The new materials have led to new shapes, but it is interesting that it is the same elements (today, massive supports, access stairs and ramps; in Rome, tiers of arches to access stairs) that are the most visible external features of the stadia. I suppose the only additional feature we now see as a requirement is extensive car parking. The Romans, living in a more densely packed city, were able to walk to their Colosseum. (We shall return to some of these points in the next section of this unit.)

To sum up, the changes seem to be of increasing size and improving facilities. Changes in materials and the extent of facilities seem to rank fairly high. The new grounds are large, and as a result expensive to build. Thus, they have an even greater impact on the town or area in which they are sited. Because there are more luxurious facilities (health suites, cafes, bars and so on), they are more expensive to build and operate. Clearly, the additional facilities mean additional sources of income and more continuous use of the structure, but it strikes me that recent developments indicate that there has been a noticeable shift 'up-market' in the design and management of football stadia. Along with this, and with the much larger buildings, has come more involvement of leading architects, and more publicity in the professional press for a type of structure that had previously been left to a few little-known specialists. Incidentally, one factor in this was a dearth of work for architects in the late 1980s as the United Kingdom passed through recession. Architects who might have considered a stadium rather beneath them under other circumstances were only too keen to take on the work. With the employment of more widely experienced architects came more imaginative and striking buildings: a sort of circular progress. The new structures are a part of, and help to bring about, changes in society. Most recently, stadia have been conceived as prestige buildings, designed not only to accommodate a football team, but to bring renown to a locality. It strikes me that there is a very similar experience here to that of the Romans who saw the first permanent amphitheatre appear in the form of the Colosseum.

5 TODAY'S COLOSSEUM? WEMBLEY STADIUM AND ITS TRADITIONS

The material in this section closely parallels the contents of TV6, and is designed to reinforce your understanding of one modern stadium and its context. You can study this either before or after the television programme, whichever is more convenient for you.

It is quite natural at a time of much stadium rebuilding that there should be great concern about a suitable national stadium. England already has a national stadium, built at Wembley in 1923, but now there are plans to rebuild it on a more luxurious and grander scale. The venture is complicated by the fact that Wembley Stadium, with its famous twin towers, is itself seen as a part of our heritage and deserving of protection. You might argue that the problem is akin to upgrading the Colosseum for modern use, although if you feel that this is a far-fetched analogy, you might consider how much updating has been needed to accommodate the regular performances of opera in the Roman amphitheatre at Verona (Figure 6.3).

This final part of Unit 6 explores the way in which a structure is designed both to accommodate functions (in this case football) and to express aspirations (in this case related to British feelings of imperial status in the 1920s). The aspirations are expressed by means of the architecture, but then the resulting structure, partly because of its status, is used to accommodate a variety of major events, and so becomes a 'venue of legends'. The venue itself, in turn, becomes a part of the consciousness of all those who are involved, as participants or spectators, in what goes on inside. Thus, the building that was designed to reflect imperial splendour colours our attitudes to Cup Finals and all the other activities that take place there; at the same time our attitude to these events colours our appreciation of the building itself. Small wonder that there was opposition to the idea of demolishing the whole structure and starting to build a new English national stadium on the site from scratch!

The context of Wembley Stadium

Wembley Stadium can seat 80,000 people and includes a dog-racing track as well as a football pitch. It is therefore one of the larger existing stadia (larger, in fact, than the Colosseum), and was designed to accommodate much more than just football. Before it was converted to an all-seater stadium it could, of course, hold even more people, as the 1923 Cup Final showed. On that occasion, so many spectators (with and without tickets) got into the ground that the match was held up for over an hour. Estimates of the numbers vary from 126,000 to 200,000 people. However, if that Cup Final is one of the more famous moments in Wembley's history, the stadium has a wider relevance to society in its use for pop and rock concerts, mass religious meetings and a range of other activities.

The stadium was built as a part of the British Empire Exhibition in 1923 (Plate 116). (You can see more of this in TV6.) Thus, like Heysel Stadium or the Colosseum, we can assume that it was intended to make a public statement as well as to provide facilities. Now that almost all the exhibition buildings have been demolished, the stadium might appear more important that it was at the time. Certainly, we need to know something about the exhibition in order to understand how and why the stadium came to be as it was.

The very concept of a British Empire Exhibition suggests a degree of national chauvinism and self-confidence. There is some confirmation of this when we learn that the idea was first suggested in 1908, just five years after a Franco-British exhibition at White City, also in London. The idea was revived after World War I, by which time national chauvinism had developed into a belief that there should be a new Commonwealth of Nations with a new faith in the future. The exhibition was consciously intended to further this idea, but three-quarters of a century later it is easier to see the emphasis on the British Empire as backward looking, even though that empire was still very much in existence in the 1920s. (Indian independence, for instance, did not take place until 1947.) We might, however, see the display of imperial might as part of a British determination to show itself as a world power. The stadium was only one part of the exhibition, and was by no means the largest building in it. The stadium covers ten acres, while the Palace of Engineering covered thirteen. Plate 114 shows the famous twin towers of the stadium in the distance beyond the equally massive Palace of Industries.

The stadium, then, was an integral part of something much larger and overtly imperial. You might feel, therefore, that the message of the buildings has quite close parallels with that of the Colosseum. It certainly had an effect on the architecture.

EXERCISE

Look at Plates 117 and 118 (Wembley, British Empire Exhibition: Palace of Industries and Stadium; Government Pavilion). What similarities can you make out between the buildings? Can you suggest reasons for the choice of style?

DISCUSSION

I hope you noticed that all the buildings make use of classical columns, although you may not have been able to identify the orders. There were also pediments and symmetrical façades, as well as examples of the British Lion, especially in the Government Pavilion. There seems to have been some effort made to establish a uniformity among these buildings and this was done using elements of the classical language of architecture. Evidently the echo of Imperial Rome was thought suitable for Imperial Britain.

The classical style was confined to the main buildings – the Government Pavilion, the Palaces of Industry and Engineering – and to the national pavilions of the developed dominions – Australia, Canada etc. The other national pavilions – Burma, India, South Africa etc. – copied the 'national' styles of their countries. You might see this as reflecting a hierarchy within the empire. The stadium uses a compromise style. There are few columns, but it makes use of arches. You may detect a distinct echo of the Colosseum (see Plate 114). However, the stadium was a different kind of building from all the national pavilions, and you can see from Figure 6.5 that it was given a special site, at one end of the main route through the exhibition.

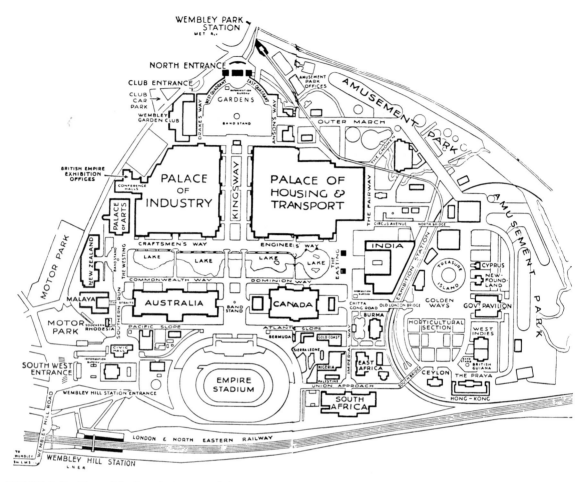

FIGURE 6.5   *Plan of the British Empire Exhibition site, 1925. (Reproduced from D. R. Knight and A. D. Sabey,* The Lion Roars at Wembley, *New Barnet, D. R. Knight, 1984, by permission of the author)*

What is Wembley Stadium? How does it fit the tradition?

The familiar view of Wembley Stadium (Plate 119) with its oversailing roof does not show the stadium as originally built. It represents two major campaigns of alteration and improvement. First, the stands were roofed in the 1960s. Then the roof was extended when the stands were made all seater and an upper tier of seats was inserted in the 1980s. However, the original building is worth studying for the way in which its designers attempted to propagandize for Britain and football.

Wembley Stadium was designed and built from the start as a single all-enclosing stadium, at a time when most football grounds had been designed piecemeal. Although there are now several single-structure stadia in the United Kingdom, its date of 1924 puts Wembley ahead of the others, just as the Colosseum was ahead in its era. I would argue that the single-structure design was part of a deliberate attempt to make

Wembley a thoroughly modern stadium. Also like the Colosseum, it is clear that Wembley was deliberately designed to appear as an outstanding building as well as to provide efficient accommodation for sport.

EXERCISE

Look at Plates 114 and 119–124 (Wembley Stadium, views and details). Can you distinguish features that are primarily for show and features that are solely for function?

DISCUSSION

The twin towers are, I think, the most obvious 'show' features, but without them Wembley would hardly be Wembley. I would also include features such as the use of a formal axial approach, the grand entrance arch, the arrangement of arched openings on the main façade and the use of a species of column with capital and base. We might wonder whether the royal box was solely to do with the function of the stadium, but that would be to raise wider questions about the function of the stadium and the nature of British society. More obviously functional is the arrangement of the interior, with its continuous terrace of seating. I think the side façade is also more functional than 'show' with its simple stairs for access, but would you include in this category the segmental arch over each of the entrances? There is certainly not as much 'show' about these as the façade arcade, but we would need more technical information to decide whether their design was governed simply by structural constraints.

I think the uncertainty that remains about some of the items is important in assessing the wider function of this structure. It is, after all, a national stadium, and this implies considerations of national prestige. This in turn is linked to developing history. The stadium built in Berlin for the 1936 Olympics (Plates 103 and 105) was deliberately intended to show the world how superior National Socialist architecture (and sport) could be. When Wembley hosted the 1948 Olympics after the war, the choice of venue was in effect a statement of the success of the countries that saw themselves as the free world. If Wembley is still to operate as the English national stadium, we need to consider whether our view of national prestige has changed since 1924, and how. There is more discussion of this aspect of the stadium and its original surroundings in TV6. On the other hand, if the stadium was built as a national symbol, it is reasonable to assume that the style and appearance were carefully planned with this in mind. We should, therefore, think about the architectural style of the building.

The architectural language of Wembley Stadium: modernity and convention

Look over the illustrations of Wembley Stadium, concentrating particularly on Plates 116, 119, 121, 122 and 124. How far do you think the stadium fits into the traditions we have been examining so far in this week's study? Does it belong most closely with the Colosseum, or with more modern stadia such as Milan Arena (Plate 125)?

DISCUSSION

I hope you can see that Milan Arena is easily recognizable as related to the Colosseum, although it does not rise as high. (It was built in 1807 and inaugurated by Napoleon, and it was used largely for military exercises. However, in 1908 it was used as a venue for international football.) I use the illustration here to remind you how strong the formal conventions of the Colosseum might be, even in the early modern period. Wembley is certainly different from Milan Arena, but I think that there are still elements of the Colosseum approach, although Wembley is, at best, a fairly distant relative. Wembley seems to me to have both elements of the classical language and of the structural modernity that was one feature of the first half of the twentieth century. The arcade of the main façade has an echo of the Colosseum, probably partly because of the similarity in the form of the two structures. There are also elements of the façade that can be called columns, in that we can recognize bases, capitals and entablatures, but these deliberately do not conform to the 'rules' of classical architecture. The arrangement of the side façades does consist of a series of arches, but they are wide segmental arches rising the full height of the building, not tiers of round-headed arches in frames as on the Colosseum. These side arches could be regarded as part of Wembley's modernity.

The clue to the difference lies in the material used. Whereas the Colosseum was built of brick and stone with concrete vaults, Wembley Stadium was built of reinforced concrete – a system not available to the Romans. Reinforced concrete had recently been developed in America, and offered both speedy and cheap construction. This was important at Wembley, where the stadium had to be built in under a year to accommodate the 1923 Cup Final. The new material had hitherto been used mostly by engineers and Wembley Stadium was, in fact, designed by an engineer, Sir Owen Williams. He designed a number of other modern structures, such as the first motorway bridges, the Boots factory in Nottingham and the Daily Express buildings in Fleet Street and Manchester. There is no attempt to conceal the structure with an appearance of columns. Rather it is displayed as a virtue in its own right, and the overall effect is of much greater lightness (particularly at the sides) than the Colosseum, although this structure is just as strong.

Why was it like that? Who did it 'speak to'?

Finally, we need to address the question of why Wembley Stadium was built in the way it was. (This discussion is further developed in TV6.)

One thought that occurs to me is that there is no necessary connection between the style or grandeur of a stadium and the quality of the activities inside. However, I think there is at least an implicit claim in the structure of Wembley Stadium that a national stadium is the most important in the country. Perhaps one reason for the use of concrete in this celebratory structure was the intention to demonstrate that the stadium was absolutely up to date. It certainly was well planned, with easy access and the full range of facilities. There is a matched pair of changing-rooms for the two teams and an on-site hospital for injuries on the field or in the crowd. The access was so well arranged that the organizers boasted that the 80,000 spectators could be evacuated in eight minutes!

However, there is also the 'show' element in the construction. This stadium has a royal box, because the high-status matches and other events held here need to be, and are, acknowledged at the highest level of society. There is, in fact, a considerable amount of space given to celebratory activity, in the shape of a huge banqueting hall and what was, when built, the longest bar in the world. The status of the stadium in relation to the whole nation is also shown in the space given to facilities for reporters, and in the provision of special railway stations specifically to bring fans from distant parts. One station opens into the far end of a straight avenue, Empire Way, now renamed Olympic Way, which links the stadium with its surrounding area and which leads directly up to the twin towers. In other words, the provision of the ornamental façade is an important part of the way in which this stadium addresses the nation.

There are, of course, less obvious assumptions about who will use which parts of the arena. The famous tunnel for the teams is functional in the extreme, and is also used for the arrival of the coaches bringing the players. The banqueting hall, bars and related areas are all carpeted, but the access stairways for the spectators, like the terraces, are left with bare concrete floors. This may originally have been suitable, in that the terraces were only roofed in 1967, but it suggests to me an assumption that the fans would accept less comfort than the VIPs. Perhaps there is a sense in which the 'show' element is allowed to dominate some of the facilities related to the purpose for which the stadium was actually designed.

One final point is that Wembley Stadium is now very much outdated. Some excellent electronic facilities have been added, including what is still the most advanced public address system in the world, but where it was possible to believe in 1924 that there was no finer stadium, it is clear that there are now many more recently built stadia that surpass Wembley. In the realm of football, as clubs in other countries became better endowed, or even more successful, than those in the United Kingdom, their stadia in Holland, Italy, South America and so on were rebuilt using the latest technology and on an increasingly lavish scale. It will be interesting to see how far the United Kingdom at the end of the twentieth century is able to go in rebuilding its national stadium.

6 CONCLUSION: ARCHITECTURE AND CULTURAL HISTORY

In this unit I have tried to introduce some key aspects of the study of architecture and its history through an examination of the form and function of a building type. I have tried to show how the language of the design of the Colosseum was developed as a means of making a massive building appear humane. I have then explored briefly the way in which architectural language has been used and adapted by architects in succeeding eras. I have also suggested some of the functional problems involved in designing stadia, and considered the sorts of solution that have been offered in recent years.

The principal justification for this approach is my belief that architecture is both interesting in itself and revealing of the aspirations and priorities of any society. This is, I believe, important in a multidisciplinary course such as A103. At one level, the history of architecture is a branch of art history. Architectural historians spend a good deal of time exploring the formal relations of one building to another and the way in which stylistic features are derived from different sources. This, however, is only one aspect of architectural history, and to understand a building fully you need to seek answers to much wider questions.

It is, perhaps, easy to see that questions of economics and of technology are important in architectural history; even politics may well be involved. After all, if there is no money there will be no building; if it does not stand up it will not function; and where emperors or national stadia are concerned the design and achievement of a building becomes a political matter on a grand scale. Yet all this falls far short of fully explaining a building. We need to be able to locate the building in the society that spawned it. This means addressing questions such as:

■ Who wanted it?

■ Who used it?

- Was it popular or successful?

- What influences were brought to bear in its realization?

- What influence did it have on society once built?

These are major questions and the answers will involve the expertise of other disciplines besides architectural history in the narrow sense. I hope, therefore, that this case study has raised some questions that interest you and perhaps made you think about some disciplines that you had not previously considered. If so, it will have helped you prepare for the study of other parts of this course.

GLOSSARY

arcade row of arches, either structural and allowing free movement between two spaces or decorative as an element of a **façade**.

architectural analysis study of the way in which the elements of a building (or part of a building) are assembled to create the complete form.

architrave name given in classical architecture to the beam that spans between columns. The lower part of the **entablature**.

articulation system of dividing or breaking up a **façade**, generally, but not always, so that it relates to the spaces and/or structure behind.

attached column when a column is used decoratively, it may function only as a part of a wall, rather than as an individual support. Often the column is built touching the wall, and it is then described as attached (or engaged). See also **half-column** and **pilaster**.

buttress structural support of a wall, designed to deflect an outward thrust from a roof. A typical feature of Gothic architecture.

cantilever system of support, common in modern architecture and frame construction, whereby a projecting element is made self-supporting by extending it inside a building so that compensating weight lies the other side of its support.

capital top element, usually decorative, of a column.

classical tradition tradition that recognizes the persistence of certain elements and shapes in buildings that can be traced back to the ancient Greek and Roman times.

colonnade row of columns supporting a beam (rather than arches – see **arcade**). Often used as an exterior feature in classical architecture.

column vertical support; in classical architecture, a part of one of the **orders**.

cornice projecting element at the top of an **order**, originally the projecting edge of a roof but transformed into a decorative element and used extensively elsewhere as well.

entablature horizontal element of a classical **order**, consisting of two parts – the **architrave** and the **frieze** – and topped by the **cornice**.

façade outer, usually front, wall of a building, often specially designed for display.

form term much used in architecture to describe the solid shape of a structure, as opposed to the space enclosed.

frieze upper part of an **entablature** corresponding to the level of the beams spanning from the **colonnade** to the wall in ancient Greek temples.

function term used in several ways to refer to the purpose of buildings or architectural elements. Buildings may have a primary function – to provide shelter; more specific functions – as dwelling/sleeping/eating spaces; or more nebulous functions – such as demonstrating the power of an individual or community. One building may combine a number of functions.

half-column when a column is used decoratively, it may function only as part of a wall, rather than as an individual support. Often the column is built as though it were embedded to half its diameter in the wall. It is then described as a half-column. Occasionally three-quarter columns are found. See also **attached column** and **pilaster**.

order technical term in the classical language of architecture that describes the column and its beam. Traditionally orders are of different designs – Doric, Ionic and Corinthian in Greek architecture – which are distinguished by both decoration and proportion.

pediment low-pitched triangular roof gable of classical buildings.

pier structural support usually rather larger than a column. Piers may be of any shape and can even be decorated with **pilasters** or attached columns.

pilaster projecting vertical strip on a wall made in the shape of a column and **capital**.

portico porch or projecting element of a building constructed with columns and, frequently, a **pediment**.

proportion system of relationships between elements of a building.

rib projecting line of masonry or brick usually spanning between two **piers** or pillars, which forms the basis of a **vault**.

scale size of a building, often related to the human form. Also the diagrammatic measure indicating the size of a building represented in a drawing.

shaft projecting line of masonry, usually rounded, which forms part of a vertical support or **pier**.

string course projecting horizontal band of masonry or brickwork marking the different stages of a **façade** or linking different elements. Most commonly used in relation to Gothic architecture (but see **cornice**).

temple frontispiece element of a wall, or wall decoration, consisting of **columns** and a **pediment**. Often the columns are attached to the wall. A common central feature in classical **façades**.

vault system of solid brick or stone roofing formed by a series of interlocking **ribs** and panels. Common in Gothic architecture and almost always covered by an outer roof.

REFERENCES

FLEMING, J., HONOUR, H. and PEVSNER, N. (1991, 4th edn) *Penguin Dictionary of Architecture*, Harmondsworth, Penguin.

SUGGESTIONS FOR FURTHER READING

You may find it interesting to look at one or more of the following:

INGLIS, S. (1990) *Football Grounds of Europe*, London, Collins/Willow.

INGLIS, S. (1996, 3rd edn) *Football Grounds of Britain*, London, Collins/Willow.

PEVSNER, N. (1960, 6th edn) *An Outline of European Architecture*, Harmondsworth, Penguin.

Sir Banister Fletcher's History of Architecture on the Comparative Method (1987, 19th edn), ed. J. Musgrove, Guildford, Butterworth.

SUMMERSON, J. (1963) *The Classical Language of Architecture*, London, BBC.

UNIT 7
READING WEEK

This is the first of a series of built-in spaces in the course, designed to help you keep up, and also consolidate and reflect on the work you've done in the preceding study weeks.

Of course, if you haven't managed to complete the first two blocks in the allocated time, it's unlikely that you'll be reading this at the beginning of a leisurely blank Study Week 7! But don't worry if it has taken you all or part of this week to complete your work on the Colosseum. Keeping up and learning how to keep up is an important study skill.

AGSG, ch.2, sects.3.4 and 5, 'Setting targets' and 'Making notes'

Suppose you did get behind. How can you learn from this experience and pace yourself better in future? Take a quick look at the volume and density of your note-taking and how much you've marked up the units. It would be very understandable if you started by making notes on everything and then tailed off. We've all gone overboard with a highlighter at some time – and discovered that marking everything just takes us back to where we started. If this has happened to you, try to take a slightly more relaxed attitude to the beginning of units or new sections. Things probably will make more sense as you go along, and any plunge into a new area can be a bit overwhelming at first. You can always go back.

Did you skip the exercises as you realized time was rushing by? That was probably not a wise move as the exercises are designed to slow you down so that a key point gets home. If you skipped and then floundered you probably lost time.

AGSG, ch.4, sect.4, 'Conclusion' and ch.5, sect.6, 'The experience of writing'

Did you spend too long on the TMA? Consult *The Arts Good Study Guide* and tell yourself that next time you're going to do *your* best not *the* best. Impossible aspirations take forever – which your tutor knows you haven't got.

Did you get interrupted too much? Try to decide whether you were (a) just distracted, (b) blown off course by a major crisis or (c) swamped by everyday life. If (a) remember that you can start work before you colour-code your paper-clips; if (b) tell your tutor. However, (c) is the tricky one because it goes on all the time: young children often get sick, washing machines break down, birthdays come round and when isn't there a rush on at work? Tell your family and friends you need a bit more space; they'll benefit if you're happier. Remember that you can let study distract you from the chores, and tell your children they are allowed to use the iron below the age of consent.

If, however, you have kept up, how best can you use this time? You might want just to catch up on your life, but don't break the successful study rhythm you have achieved. Try to put in at least ten hours during this week. It's probably not a good idea to re-read everything at top speed. Ask yourself what you've found most rewarding and what most demanding, and go back to both. You may already be sure that some subjects are not for you, but don't give up just because you found something particularly difficult. After all, you committed yourself to an intellectual challenge when you undertook the course.

A103 is designed to help you make informed choices among all the options available for future study in the Arts Faculty, but it isn't wise to exclude any option too soon, not least because the popular interdisciplinary arts courses call for a full range of skills. In this Foundation Course, the disciplines are linked in various interdependent combinations so that if, for example, you left out the next literature unit in Block 5 (*Pygmalion*) you would put yourself at a disadvantage with the Classical Studies text *Medea*. So if you are already making choices, plan to give one or two disciplines *less* attention rather than leaving them out altogether.

Last but not least, there is a television programme scheduled for this week, TV7, *Passing Judgement*, which is designed to build on and develop the work you have just completed. Programmes are also scheduled for viewing in the reading weeks to follow. Details of how to get the most out of these programmes will be found in the Broadcast Notes.

INDEX TO BLOCK 2

This index includes references to the Colour Plates and Plates in the *Illustration Book*; these are indicated by 'CPl.' for Colour Plates and 'Pl.' for Plates.

AN INTRODUCTION TO THE HUMANITIES